Favorite Novenas and Prayers

*compiled and edited
by
Norma Cronin Cassidy*

PAULIST PRESS
New York/Mahwah

NIHIL OBSTAT:
Rev. Charles W. Gusmer
Censor Librorum

IMPRIMATUR:
✠Thomas A. Boland
Archbishop of Newark

September 29, 1972

Library of Congress Cataloging-in-Publication Data
Favorite novenas and prayers/compiled and edited by Norma
    Cronin Cassidy.—Rev. ed.
        p.   cm.
    ISBN 0-8091-3205-2
    1. Novenas.   2. Catholic Church—Prayer-books and de-
votions—English.   I. Cassidy, Norma Cronin.
BX2170.N7F38   1990
242'.802—dc20   90-36453
                                                     CIP

Published by Paulist Press
997 Macarthur Boulevard
Mahwah, New Jersey 07430

Printed and bound in the
United States of America

Contents

GENERAL PRAYERS

Foreword

When at the Last Supper Christ gave himself to his apostles under the form of bread and wine, there took place the identification he talked about in the sixth chapter of St. John. "He that eateth my flesh and drinketh my blood abideth in me and I in him." This identification went in two directions: the apostles acquired a new family background in the life of God; Christ took upon himself the iniquity of us all.

Since the family life of God and the sinful life of the family of men are incompatible, one had to go.

So Christ died on the Cross, taking down with him into the ground the sin which touched his sinlessness in the Eucharistic identification. The apostles, and all of us, died with him. So did sin lose its hold on us.

When Our Lord, and we with him, rose from the dead the new family background of the redeemed was the same as that of God's own Son. We live now and operate as one who has his roots in heaven.

The resurrection is the visibility of all this.

There have been many resurrections since that first on Easter morning. One of them is this little collection of novenas and prayers which Norma Cassidy has collected for us in the present volume.

With all that has happened since Vatican II many things long associated with devotions and liturgy in the Church have died; their defects or shortcomings, their out-of-dateness dying with them. There was nothing wrong with them (no sin in them) save their inability to weather the way of the Cross which the Church has been going through, to die to a life which was of the past, so as to live in a growing world still to be redeemed.

These novenas and prayers have now risen from the dead. They come to us with the vigor of a resurrection because all that is in them is imperishable, and full of the life of heaven. Only the best survive.

Thomas H. Moore, S.J.

Daily
Prayers

The Our Father

Our Father, who art in heaven, hallowed be your name; your kingdom come; your will be done on earth as it is in heaven. Give us this day our daily bread; and forgive us our trespasses as we forgive those who trespass against us; and lead us not into temptation; but deliver us from evil. Amen.

The Hail Mary

Hail Mary, full of grace, the Lord is with you; blessed are you among women, and blessed is the fruit of your womb, Jesus. Holy Mary, mother of God, pray for us sinners now and at the hour of our death. Amen.

The Apostles' Creed

I believe in God, the Father Almighty, maker of heaven and earth and in Jesus Christ, his only Son, our Lord; who was conceived by the Holy Spirit, born of the Virgin Mary, suffered under Pontius Pilate; was crucified; died and was buried. He descended into hell, the third day he arose again from the dead; he ascended into heaven, sits at the right hand of God, the Father Almighty; from thence he shall come to judge the living and the dead. I believe in the Holy Spirit, the holy Catholic Church, the communion of saints, the forgiveness of sins, the resurrection of the body, and life everlasting. Amen.

The Confiteor

I confess to Almighty God; to blessed Mary, ever virgin, to blessed Michael the Archangel; to blessed John the Baptist; to the holy apostles Peter and Paul, and to all the saints, that I have sinned exceedingly in thought, word and deed, through my fault, through my most grievous fault. Therefore I beseech blessed Mary, ever virgin, blessed Michael the archangel, blessed John the Baptist, the holy apostles Peter and Paul, and all the saints, to pray to the Lord our God for me.

May the Almighty God have mercy on me, forgive me my sins, and bring me to everlasting life. Amen.

May the Almighty and Merciful Lord grant me pardon, absolution, and remission of all my sins. Amen.

Act of Faith

O my God, I firmly believe that you are one God in three Divine Persons, Father, Son and Holy Spirit; I believe that your Divine Son became man, and died for our sins, and that he will come to judge the living and the dead. I believe these and all the truths that the holy Catholic Church teaches because you have revealed them, who can neither deceive nor be deceived. Amen.

Act of Hope

O my God, relying on your infinite goodness and promises, I hope to obtain pardon of my sins, the help of your grace, and life everlasting, through the merits of Jesus Christ, my Lord and Redeemer. Amen.

Act of Love

O my God, I love you above all things, with my whole heart and soul, because you are all good and worthy of all my love. I love my neighbor as myself for love of you. I forgive all who have injured me and ask pardon of all whom I have injured.

Act of Contrition

O my God, I am heartily sorry for having offended you and I detest all my sins because I dread the loss of heaven and the pains of hell, but most of all because they offend you, my God, who are all good and deserving of all my love. I firmly resolve with the help of your grace, to confess my sins, to do penance and to amend my life. Amen.

The Memorare

Remember, O most gracious Virgin Mary, that never was it known that anyone who fled to your protection, implored your help, and sought your intercession, was left unaided. Inspired with this confidence, I fly unto you, O virgin of virgins, my mother! To you I come, before you I stand sinful and sorrowful. O Mother of the Word Incarnate, despise not my petition, but in your mercy hear and answer me. Amen.

Prayer to St. Michael

St. Michael, the archangel, defend us in battle; be our protection against the malice and snares of the devil. We humbly beseech you, O God, to command him and do you, O prince of the heavenly host, by the divine power, cast into hell Satan and all the other evil spirits who roam through the world seeking the destruction of souls. Amen.

Glory Be to the Father

Glory be to the Father, and to the Son, and to the Holy Spirit. As it was in the beginning is now, and ever shall be, world without end. Amen.

Prayer to St. Raphael the Archangel

Glorious Archangel, St. Raphael, great prince of the heavenly court, you are illustrious for your gifts of wisdom and grace. You are a guide of those who journey by land, or sea, or air, consoler of the afflicted, and refuge of sinners. I beg you, assist me in all my needs and in all the sufferings of this life, as once you helped the young Tobias on his travels. Because you are the "medicine of God" I humbly pray you to heal the many infirmities of my soul and the ills that afflict my body. I especially ask of you the favor (*name it*) and the great grace of purity to prepare me to be the temple of the Holy Spirit. Amen.

Morning Offering

O Jesus, through the immaculate heart of Mary, I offer you my prayers, works, joys and sufferings of this day, for all the intentions of your Sacred Heart, in union with the Holy Sacrifice of the Mass throughout the world, in reparation for my sins, and for the general intention recommended for this month. Amen.

Novenas

Novena to the Sacred Heart

O Divine Jesus who has said, "Ask and you shall receive; seek and you shall find, knock and it shall be opened to you," behold me prostrate at your feet. Animated with a lively faith and confidence in the promises dictated by your Sacred Heart and pronounced by your adorable lips, I come to ask your aid (*here mention your request*).

From whom shall I ask, O sweet Jesus, if not from you whose heart is an inexhaustible source of all graces and merits? Where shall I seek if not from the treasure which contains all the riches of your clemency and bounty? Where shall I knock if it be not at the door of your Sacred Heart through which God himself comes to us and through which we go to God?

To you then, O Heart of Jesus, I have recourse. In you I find consolation when afflicted, protection when persecuted, strength when overwhelmed with trials and light in doubt and darkness. I firmly believe you can bestow on me the grace I implore even though it should require a miracle. You have only to will it and my prayer will be granted. I know I am most unworthy of your favors, O Jesus, but this is not a reason for me to be discouraged. You are the God of mercies and you will not refuse a contrite and humble heart. Cast upon me a look of pity, I conjure you, and your compassionate Heart will find in my miseries and weakness a pressing motive for granting my petition.

But, O Sacred Heart, whatever may be your decision with regard to my request I will never cease to adore, love, praise and serve you. Deign, O Jesus, to accept my act of perfect submission to the decrees of your adorable Heart which I sincerely desire may be fulfilled in and by me and all your creatures forever and ever. Amen.

Act of Consecration to the Sacred Heart of Jesus

Most sweet Jesus, redeemer of the human race look down upon us humbly prostrate before your altar. We are yours and yours we wish to be but to be more surely united with you behold each one of us freely consecrates himself today to your most Sacred Heart. Many indeed have never known you, many too, despising your precepts have rejected you. Have mercy on them all, most merciful Jesus, and draw them to your Sacred Heart.

Be you king, O Lord, not only of the faithful who have never forsaken you but also of the prodigal children who have abandoned you. Grant that they may quickly return to their Father's house lest they die of wretchedness and hunger.

Be you King of those who are deceived by erroneous opinions or whom discord keeps aloof and call them back to the harbor of truth and the unity of faith so that soon there may be but one flock and one shepherd.

Grant, O Lord, to your Church assurance of freedom and immunity from harm. Give peace and order to all nations and make the earth resound from pole to pole with one cry: Praise to the Divine Heart that wrought our salvation; to it be glory and honor forever. Amen.

Special Prayer for Each Day

FIRST DAY

My God and my Lord, Jesus Christ, in deepest humility I kneel before you and adore your Divine Heart. No one dares to doubt that you will grant all graces necessary to our salvation. Did you not say: "God alone is good," and are not you my very God? Is not your Heart the Heart of God who is all love?

Therefore, there can be no power that is able to hinder you from granting our requests. Nothing is difficult for your omnipotence and your riches are infinite and can never be exhausted.

No matter how often I may have sinned against you, I shall not despair because I know that you are God, infinite in generosity and mercy, always ready to pardon every contrite and humble sinner.

O compassionate Heart of Jesus, God of solace, grant me comfort. Pardon me, come to my assistance. Say but the word and I shall find relief in my sore trials.

I place my hope in you. Let me not be confounded. O Heart of my omnipotent God, have mercy on me.

SECOND DAY

With the greatest confidence I come to you, the fatherly Heart of Jesus for I know that no father, were he ever so loving and solicitous, can possibly love his children as you have always loved me. To whom, therefore, shall I go if not to you the best of fathers and the author of all good? It is indeed true that I have grievously offended you, that I have neglected to honor you properly and have been guilty of ingratitude and do not deserve to be numbered among your children. But although I forgot my duty to you as your child I know that you are still my beloved Father in heaven. Now with a contrite heart I kneel at your feet weeping over my sins and promising you that in the future I shall make every effort never to offend you again. I hope in spite of my sinfulness to be received by you who have so often sought me. O sweetest Heart of Jesus help me with your grace so that I may carry out my resolution. Then, O Jesus, if my wishes are not contrary to your most holy will, I beg of you (*mention your favor*) for which I pray with confidence and hope to receive from your infinite goodness.

THIRD DAY

O beloved Jesus, my heart is deeply moved at the thought that you, Almighty God, should take upon yourself our human nature in order to enable you to become our brother and to make us children of God. But your loving Heart was not satisfied to raise us to such high dignity; you also desired to make us partakers in your inheritance in the kingdom of heaven. How greatly are we indebted to you for these favors. O how I grieve to think that until this very day I have been so ungrateful for your many gifts. Most humbly do I ask for your forgiveness and pray that you will through the merits of your Sacred Heart grant me the grace to follow you in all things so that at death your heavenly Father may find me worthy to be your brother in heaven. Furthermore, I beg of your most merciful Heart to have pity on me in my present need and grant me the favor (*name it*) that I hope to obtain from you.

FOURTH DAY

O sweetest Heart of Jesus, to whom shall I turn in all my sorrows if not to you, the faithful friend of our souls? You have given your very life for me. How then can you refuse me your assistance during my life? It is true, indeed, and I must confess this to you, that instead of relying on you only I have too often trusted to the love and friendship of creatures although I had frequently experienced their treachery. If I have thus insulted you in the past, I promise in the future never to repeat the offense. I promise henceforth in all my doubts, afflictions and needs I will have recourse to you only to find light, help, comfort and grace. Henceforth, you alone shall be my friend, upon you alone will I rely. Your friendship shall be above all others. In fact, I promise to renounce all other friendships if they are an occasion of disloyalty to you. To manifest my perfect trust in you, I now beg of you to help me in my present need (*name it*).

I pray you to be my "strong defense." Be to me a "medicine for immortality." By kindly granting this request, you will unite my heart more closely with yours and make me forever grateful for your love. Do not permit my trust in you to be confounded, O eternally faithful, benevolent and sweet Heart of Jesus.

FIFTH DAY

O Divine Savior, the infinite love of your Sacred Heart was so inflamed for us that it brought you as a sacrifice of propitiation for our sins to the altar of the cross. Still your love was not satisfied with this but permitted your Heart to be opened with a lance that through this wound we might behold the innermost love of this heart and better understand your indescribable longing for our salvation. You have given us the wounded Heart and kept it open not only that we might find therein a protection against the justice of the Eternal Father whom we have offended by our sins but also that this source of grace and mercy may always be open to us in our needs. Why then do I come to you so seldom and so indifferently? Why do I not fly to this source of all grace? O dearest Jesus forgive me these insults which through want of confidence in you I have so often committed against you. Behold, I now come to you with living faith with the intention never to leave you. Here I shall seek what I need so much, first the forgiveness of my sins, the grace to do better, and then I pray for your assistance in my present need (*name it*).

SIXTH DAY

O Jesus, my divine model and teacher, what can I do when I see you the Son of the Eternal Father, full of glory and honor, laden with the cross, walking the awful road to death, especially when thereby you show me the way to salvation without selfishness but only for my benefit? O Jesus, what can I do but have faith in you and return your love by at least bearing my trials in patience and humility. And this, particularly, my God, because I have so often experienced the great power that my passions have over me, and how seldom I can withstand the temptations of the world. How hard do I not find it to deny myself the pleasure to mortify my desires and to renounce the false splendor of the world although I know full well that all these things so easily lead me into sin. O give me strength to resist my passions and close my eyes to the allurements and charms of the world, help me to imitate your poverty, purity and humility, and send me trials with the strength to bear them humbly. Though I fear them, they are necessary for me. But I wish to follow you and become like you. Therefore, permit me to drink all of your chalice of suffering. Heart of Jesus, burning for love of me, inflame my heart with love for you. Amen.

SEVENTH DAY

O my Divine Savior, according to the words of the Holy Scriptures, you are in truth our advocate before your Father. You have freely taken this office upon yourself and unceasingly exercise it with faithful and loving zeal for all who trust in you. Your influence with the Father is so great he will not refuse you. He always hears you as you have testified at the grave of Lazarus. Filled with this faith and with confidence in your compassionate Heart I come to you to plead my cause. I have offended your Father and have called the anger of his Majesty upon myself. I am heavily indebted to his strict justice. I have nothing with which to pay the debt and therefore must fear the punishment. Besides all this, I am in the present need of . . . where only the power of the Father can help me. For the salvation of my soul I sorely need this grace. O may it come to me from the riches of your Father. O my beloved advocate, from your throne in heaven to your Father and to my Father, to your God and to my God, reconcile me with him. Repay my debts out of the infinite treasury of your merits and obtain for me assistance in my present trial and the grace that I need so much. In the "Our Father" you have composed a prayer with which I will now approach the Father. Accompany me and with the fervor and power of your most Sacred Heart as my mediator, say with me: Our Father, who are in heaven. . . .

EIGHTH DAY

My God and my Savior, Jesus Christ, I believe it to be an undeniable truth. I believe it firmly, O Jesus, that you are my good shepherd. Even if you had not said it, I would believe it because I know that you have in my behalf always manifested the heart of a good shepherd. Would that I, during my entire life, had permitted the goodness and solicitude of your Heart to lead me; would that I had never departed from your side, for then I would not have suffered so much misery and tribulation. But alas, I was untrue to you so often that in consequence I fell into the abyss of sin and was mortally wounded. Now, however, your straying lamb calls to you from the depths of its misery. O my good Shepherd, have mercy on me; give me proof again of your compassionate Heart. After all that you have thus far done for me I cannot believe that your Heart will reject me. Consequently, I beseech this Heart, I embrace it with confidence; and conjure you by all your merits that you obtain for me from your heavenly Father the forgiveness of my sins and the grace for a complete conversion. And then I also pray for the grace of . . . which I am so much in need and which I hope to receive as the fruit of this novena. O Heart of the good Shepherd, have mercy on me. Amen.

NINTH DAY

O adorable Savior, Jesus Christ, I believe what your holy Word teaches. I believe that you were made a priest forever by the solemn oath of your eternal Father and that you offer sacrifices forever. I believe that you offer the most sublime, holy and pure sacrifice most pleasing to God in the fire of your love, your Heart, your infinite merits, even your entire self. I believe that the most profound compassion of your priestly Heart impels you to carry on the function of your priesthood forever and ever in order to reconcile your Father with us and to offer him adoration, praise and thanksgiving for us as well as to entreat him and grant us every needed grace.

Inspired by this faith I come to you, O loving Jesus. I place all my needs with great confidence in your priestly Heart and upon the altar of your Heart. The eternal Father cannot refuse anything to such a priest and his sacrifice. Remember me then in all the Masses in which you offer yourself today throughout the world. Let your petition ascend from your Sacred Heart that the eternal Father may decide, through your merits, to forgive me all my sins which I detest from the bottom of my heart and in his fatherly love to grant me the grace for which I have so ardently pleaded during this novena. . . . O Sacred Heart, if the heavenly Father grants this request for your sake it will redound to your own glory because it will be a testimony to your Father's love for you. Procure this honor for yourself and from the sanctuary of heaven bring to me this desired grace so that my faith in you may be strengthened and my love of you may be more enkindled, O loving and priestly Heart of Jesus.

Litany of the Sacred Heart

Lord, have mercy on us.
Christ, have mercy on us.
Lord, have mercy on us.
Christ, hear us.
Christ, graciously hear us.

God, the Father of Heaven,*
God, the Son, Redeemer of
  the world,

------
* *Have mercy on us.*

God, the Holy Spirit,

Holy Trinity, one God,

Heart of Jesus, Son of the Eternal Father,

Heart of Jesus, formed by the Holy Spirit in the womb of the Virgin Mother,

Heart of Jesus, substantially united to the Word of God,

Heart of Jesus, of Infinite Majesty,

Heart of Jesus, Sacred Temple of God,

Heart of Jesus, Tabernacle of the Most High,

Heart of Jesus, House of God and Gate of Heaven,

Heart of Jesus, burning furnace of charity,

Heart of Jesus, abode of Justice and Love,

Heart of Jesus, full of Goodness and Love,

Heart of Jesus, abyss of all virtues,

Heart of Jesus, most worthy of all praise,

Heart of Jesus, King and Center of all hearts,

Heart of Jesus, in whom are all the treasures of wisdom and knowledge,

Heart of Jesus, in whom dwells the fullness of divinity,

Heart of Jesus, in whom the Father was well pleased,

Heart of Jesus, of whose fullness we have all received.

Heart of Jesus, desire of the everlasting hills,

Heart of Jesus, patient and most merciful,

Heart of Jesus, enriching all who invoke Thee,

Heart of Jesus, fountain of life and holiness,

Heart of Jesus, propitiation of our sins,

Heart of Jesus, loaded down with opprobrium,

Heart of Jesus, bruised for our offenses,

Heart of Jesus, obedient unto death,

Heart of Jesus, pierced with a lance,

Heart of Jesus, source of all consolation,

Heart of Jesus, our life and resurrection,

Heart of Jesus, our peace and reconciliation,

Heart of Jesus, victim of sin,

Heart of Jesus, salvation of those who trust in you,

Heart of Jesus, hope of those who die in you,

Heart of Jesus, delight of all the saints,

Lamb of God, who takes away the sins of the world, *spare us, O Lord.*

Lamb of God, who takes away the sins of the world, *graciously hear us, O Lord.*
Lamb of God, who takes away the sins of the world, *have mercy on us.*

Jesus meek and humble of heart,
Make our hearts like unto Thine.

Let Us Pray

O Almighty and Eternal God, look upon the Heart of your dearly beloved Son and upon the praise and satisfaction he offers you in behalf of sinners, and, being appeased, grant pardon to those who seek your mercy in the name of the same Jesus Christ, your Son, who lives and reigns with you in the unity of the Holy Spirit, world without end. Amen.

Act of Reparation

O Heart of Jesus, whose overflowing charity for men is requited by so much forgetfulness, negligence and contempt, behold us prostrate before your altar, eager to repair by a special act of homage the cruel indifference and injuries to which your loving Heart is everywhere subject.

Mindful, alas, that we ourselves have had a share in such great indignities, which we now deplore from the depths of our hearts, we humbly ask your pardon and declare our readiness to atone by voluntary expiation not only for our own personal offenses; but also for the sins of those who, straying far from the path of salvation, refuse in their obstinate infidelity to follow you, their Shepherd and Leader, or, renouncing the vows of their Baptism, have cast off the sweet yoke of your law.

We are now resolved to expiate each and every deplorable outrage committed against you; we are determined to make amends for the manifold offenses against Christian modesty in unbecoming dress and behavior, for all the foul seductions laid to ensnare the feet of the innocent, for the frequent violation of Sundays and holy-days, and the shocking blasphemies uttered against you and your Saints. We wish also to make amends for the insults to which your Vicar on earth and your priests are subjected, for the profanation by conscious neglect or terrible acts of sacrilege, of the very Sacrament of your divine love; and lastly for the public crimes of nations, who resist the rights and teaching authority of the Church which you have founded.

Would, O Divine Jesus, we were able to wash away such abominations with our blood. We now offer, in reparation for these violations of your divine honor, the satisfaction you once made to your eternal Father on the Cross and which you continue to renew daily on our altars; we offer it in union with the acts of atonement of your Virgin Mother and all the saints and of the pious faithful on earth; and we sincerely promise to make recompense, as far as we can with the help of your grace, for all neglect of your great love and for the sins we and others have committed in the past. Henceforth, we will live a life of unwavering faith, of purity of conduct, of perfect observance of the precepts of the Gospel and especially that of charity. We promise to the best of our ability to prevent others from offending you and to bring as many as possible to follow you.

O loving Jesus, through the intercession of the

23

Blessed Virgin Mary, our model in reparation, deign to receive the voluntary offering we make of this act of expiation; and by the crowning gift of perseverance keep us faithful unto death in our duty and the allegiance we owe to you, so that we may one day come to that happy home, where you with the Father and the Holy Spirit live and reign, God, world without end. Amen.

Petition to the Sacred Heart

O Sacred Heart of Jesus, I have asked you for many favors but I plead for this one (*here mention request*). Take it, place it in your open, broken Heart, and when the Eternal Father sees it covered with the mantle of your most Precious Blood, he will not refuse it. It is not my prayer, but yours. O Sacred Heart of Jesus, I place all my trust in you.

For the Souls in Purgatory

O Divine Heart of Jesus, grant, we beseech you, eternal rest to the souls in purgatory, the final grace to those who shall die today, true repentance to sinners, the light of faith to pagans and your blessing to me and mine.

Novena to the Holy Spirit

Hymn:
Come, Holy Ghost

Come, Holy Ghost, Creator blest!
And in our souls take up your rest;
Come with your grace and heavenly aid
To fill the hearts which you have made;
To fill the hearts which you have made.

O Comforter! to you we cry,
Our heavenly gift of God most High;
Our fount of life and fire of love,
And sweet anointing from above;
And sweet anointing from above.

Novena Prayer

O Holy Spirit, divine Consoler! I adore you as my
true God. I bless you by uniting myself to the praises
you receive from the angels and the saints. I offer you
my whole heart, and I render you heartfelt thanks for

all the benefits you have bestowed and do unceasingly bestow upon the world. You who are the author of all supernatural gifts and who did enrich with immense favors the soul of the Blessed Virgin Mary, the Mother of God, I beseech you to visit me by your grace and your love, and grant me the favor I so earnestly seek in this novena.... O Holy Spirit, spirit of truth, come into our hearts: shed the brightness of your light on all nations, that they may be one in faith and pleasing to you. Amen.

Come, O Holy Spirit, fill the hearts of your faithful, and kindle in them the fire of your love.

FIRST DAY

O Holy Spirit, bestow upon us your seven holy gifts. Enlighten our understanding that we may know you. Give us wisdom that your will may be clear to us and that we may accept it. Grant us the gift of counsel that we may always perceive what is right. Fortify us that we may always be capable of fulfilling your divine will. Inspire us with the spirit of learning that we may be able to penetrate more deeply into the truths that you have revealed. Let our hearts be steeped in the spirit of childlikeness that we may bring you joy. Let us have a proper fear of God that we may never grieve you or wander from the path of goodness. Give us the fullness of your gifts that we may glorify you. Amen.

Look with compassion upon us, O Holy Spirit, and grant us the favor we seek in this novena ... if it be in accordance with your holy will.

SECOND DAY

O Holy Spirit, make me faithful in every thought, and grant that I may always listen to your voice, and watch for your light, and follow your gracious inspirations. I cling to you, and give myself to you, and ask you by your compassion to watch over me in my weakness. Holding the pierced feet of Jesus, looking at his five wounds, trusting in his precious blood, adoring his opened side and stricken heart, I implore you, adorable Spirit, helper of my infirmity, to keep me in your grace, now and always, and grant us the favor we ask in this novena. . . . Amen.

Come, O Holy Spirit, fill the hearts of your faithful, and kindle in them the fire of your love.

THIRD DAY

Heavenly Father, you have called me to be a member of the mystical body of your Son, Jesus Christ, and to be a temple of the Holy Spirit. I ask you to give me these gifts of the Holy Spirit: wisdom, that I may understand the follies of this world; understanding, that I may grasp more fully the meaning of my existence and the purpose of all things in the world; counsel, that I may always choose the proper way; fortitude, that I may remain faithful to you under the pressure of temptation; piety, that I may revere you in all I do, think, or say; fear of the Lord, that should the motive of love fail me, I may be quickly awakened to the eternal consequences of my deeds.

Visit me by your grace and your love and grant me the favor I so earnestly seek in this novena. . . . Amen.

Come, O Holy Spirit, fill the hearts of your faithful, and kindle in them the fire of your love.

FOURTH DAY

O God, who today by the light of the Holy Spirit did instruct the hearts of the faithful, give us, by the light of the same Holy Spirit, a love for what is right and just and a constant enjoyment of his comforts. Pray, O Holy Spirit, that I may strive to learn more of my faith; that I may ever be conscious that reason in all its human magnificence is capable of grasping but a glimpse of the reality that is God. Pray that I may accept as the motto of my life: "All for the greater glory of God" and grant me the favor I so earnestly seek in this novena. . . . Amen.

Come, O Holy Spirit, fill the hearts of your faithful, and kindle in them the fire of your love.

FIFTH DAY

Come, O Spirit of sanctity, from the glory of heaven and send forth the radiance of your light. Father of all the poor, light and peace of all hearts, come with your countless gifts. Consoler in desolation; refreshment full of loveliness, come, dear friend of my soul. In weariness send repose; breathe gently the cool refreshing breeze; console the desolate who weep alone. O Light of beatitude, make our hearts ready;

come enter into our souls. Without your grace, man stands alone; he cannot be good or sure. Cleanse what is soiled; heal what is wounded; moisten what is arid. Bend the stubborn will; warm the cold heart; guide the wandering footstep. O Holy Spirit, we beg you to give us grace through your sevenfold power and grant me the favor I so earnestly seek in this novena. . . . Give us merit for the present, and one day beatitude when we have finished our earthly journey. Amen.

Come, O Holy Spirit, fill the hearts of your faithful, and kindle in them the fire of your love.

SIXTH DAY

O Father in heaven, I beg you to send the Holy Spirit. May your Holy Spirit remind me when I am apt to forget your law, your love, your promises. May your Holy Spirit strengthen my memory to recall frequently your sanctity, omniscience, wisdom and goodness, faithfulness and love. May your Holy Spirit encourage me when I am slothful; strengthen me when I am weak; enlighten me when I no longer can help myself. Breathe into me, O Holy Spirit, that my mind may turn to what is holy. Move me, that I may do what is holy. Stir me, that I may love what is holy. Strengthen me, that I may preserve what is holy. Protect me, Holy Spirit, that I may never lose what is holy and grant me the favor I so earnestly seek in this novena. . . . Amen.

Come, O Holy Spirit, fill the hearts of your faithful, and kindle in them the fire of your love.

Come, Holy Spirit, creator of all things: come, visit our hearts with your power. Fill with grace, friendly guest, the hearts which you have created. You are called the Consoler, gift from the hand of God, source of life, light, love, and flame, highest good. You are the pledge of sevenfold grace, finger of the Father's hand, promised us by him, and you make our tongues speak the truth. Cast light on our senses, pour love into our hearts. Grant our weak bodies strength that they may never grow weary of doing good and grant me the favor I so earnestly seek in this novena. . . . Keep the enemy far from us, give us peace always, let us willingly follow in your footsteps that we may be far removed from sin. Grant that through you we may grow in knowledge of the Father and of the Son, and that we may ever strongly believe in you, the Spirit of both. Praise and honor be forever to the Father on the highest throne, in the risen Son of God, in the Consoler. Amen.

Come, O Holy Spirit, fill the hearts of your faithful, and kindle in them the fire of your love.

EIGHTH DAY

O Holy Spirit, life and light of the Church, give us thoughts higher than our own thoughts, and prayers better than our own prayers, and powers beyond our own powers, that we may love and live, imitating Jesus Christ, our Lord and Savior. Come to us, Holy

Spirit, come with the Father and the Son and grant me the favor I so earnestly seek in this novena. . . . Vouchsafe to dwell within our souls and quickly make our hearts your own. Quench in us the fires of hate and strife, the wasting fever of the heart. From perils guard our feeble life and to our souls your peace impart. Let voice and mind and heart and strength confess and glorify your name and let the fire of charity burn bright and other hearts inflame. Amen.

Come, O Holy Spirit, fill the hearts of your faithful, and kindle in them the fire of your love.

NINTH DAY

O Lord, Holy Spirit, grant me sight to see the wondrous promise of divine love; insight to see my own weakness; delight in your divine presence in my soul which you have made your temple through sanctifying grace. I pray, O Holy Spirit, that I be not doubting; that I be spared the pain of being alone without trust or hope in Christ; that my prayer may always be "My Lord and my God!" I pray that I may acquire a sense of retreat to prayer and recollection at various times in my daily life; for prayer is the bond that joins us to Christ. I pray that I may be aware of the physical needs of the poor and that I may share what I can with them in the charitable works of the Church. I pray, O Holy Spirit, that you will in your mercy grant me the favor I have sought in this novena. . . . Amen.

Come, O Holy Spirit, fill the hearts of your faithful, and kindle in them the fire of your love.

"He who asks of God in faith things needed for this life is sometimes mercifully heard and sometimes mercifully not heard. For the physician knows better than the patient what will avail for the sick man."

Holy Spirit, Lord of Light,
From Thy throne in splendor bright
Shed on us a ray divine;
Come and from Thy boundless store
On our hearts Thy treasures pour;
Come and make us truly Thine.

O Thou blessed light divine,
Shine within these hearts of Thine,
And our inmost being fill!

Heal our wounds: our strength renew;
On our dryness pour Thy dew;
Wash our stains of guilt away;
Bend and sway our stubborn will;
From our hearts remove the chill;
Guide our footsteps when we stray.

Novena to St. Jude

St. Jude, glorious apostle, faithful servant and friend of Jesus, the name of the traitor has caused you to be forgotten by many. But the Church honors and invokes you universally as the patron of hopeless cases, and of things despaired of. Pray for me who am so distressed. Make use, I implore you, of that particular privilege accorded you to bring visible and speedy help where help was almost despaired of. Come to my assistance in this great need that I may receive the consolation and succor of heaven in all my necessities, tribulations and sufferings particularly . . . (*here make your request*) and that I may bless God with you and all the elect throughout eternity. St. Jude, apostle, martyr and relative of our Lord Jesus Christ, of Mary and of Joseph, intercede for us! Amen.

Special Prayers for Each Day

FIRST DAY

O blessed apostle St. Jude, who labored so zealously among the Gentiles in many lands, and performed numerous miracles in needy and despairing cases, we invoke you to take a special interest in us and our needs. We feel that you understand us in a particular way. Hear our prayers and our petitions and plead for us in all our necessities especially . . . . May we be patient in learning God's holy will and courageous in carrying it out. Amen.

St. Jude, pray for us!

My Jesus, mercy!

SECOND DAY

O blessed apostle Jude, who has been instrumental in gathering us here together this day, grant us that we may always serve Jesus Christ as he deserves to be served, giving of our best efforts in living as he wishes us to live. May we so dispose our hearts and minds that God will always be inclined to listen to our prayers and petitions, especially those petitions which we entrust to your care and for which we ask you to plead for us. . . .

Grant that we may be enlightened as to what is best for us, in the present and future, not forgetting the blessings we have received in the past. Amen.

St. Jude, pray for us!

My Jesus, mercy!

THIRD DAY

O holy St. Jude, apostle of Jesus Christ, you who have so faithfully and devotedly helped to spread his Gospel of Light, we who are gathered together today in your honor, ask and petition you to remember us and our needs. Especially do we pray for . . . . May it also please our Lord to lend an ear to your supplications in our behalf. Grant that we may ever pray with fervor and devotion, resigning ourselves humbly to the divine will, seeing God's purpose in all our trials and knowing that he will leave no sincere prayer unanswered in some way. Amen.

St. Jude, pray for us!

My Jesus, mercy!

FOURTH DAY

St. blessed Jude, you were called to be one of Christ's chosen apostles and labored to bring men to a knowledge and love of God; listen with compassion to those gathered together to honor you and ask your intercession. In this troubled world of ours we have many trials, difficulties and temptations. Plead for us in the heavenly court, asking that our petitions may be answered, especially the particular one we have in mind at this moment. . . . May it please God to answer our prayers in the way that he knows best, giving us grace to see his purpose in all things. Amen.

St. Jude, pray for us!

My Jesus, mercy!

FIFTH DAY

O holy St. Jude, apostle and companion of Jesus Christ, you have shown us by example how to lead a life of zeal and devotion. We humbly entreat you today to hear our prayers and petitions. Especially do we ask you to obtain for us the following favor. . . .

Grant that in praying for present and future favors we may not forget the innumerable ones granted in the past but often return to give thanks. Humbly we resign ourselves to God's holy will, knowing that he alone knows what is best for us especially in our present needs and necessities. Amen.

St. Jude, pray for us!

My Jesus, mercy!

SIXTH DAY

St. Jude, apostle of Christ and helper in despairing cases, hear the prayers and petitions of those who are gathered together in your honor. In all our needs and desires may we only seek what is pleasing to God and what is best for our salvation. These, our petitions . . . we submit to you, asking you to obtain them for us, if they are for the good of our souls. We are resigned to God's holy will in all things, knowing that he will leave no sincere prayer unanswered in some way though it may be in a way unexpected by us. Amen.

St. Jude, pray for us!

My Jesus, mercy!

SEVENTH DAY

O holy apostle St. Jude, in whose honor we are gathered today, may we never forget that our Lord and Savior Jesus Christ chose you to be one of his twelve apostles. Because of this and of the martyrdom you suffered for the Faith, we know you are a close friend of Almighty God. Therefore we do not hesitate to

36

petition you in our necessities, especially. . . . We humbly submit ourselves to the will of God, knowing full well that no sincere prayer is ever left unanswered. May we see God's good and gracious purpose working in all our trials. Amen.

St. Jude, pray for us!

My Jesus, mercy!

EIGHTH DAY

O holy St. Jude, apostle of Christ, pray that we may ever imitate the Divine Master and live according to his will. May we cooperate with the grace of God and ever remain pleasing in his sight. Especially do we ask you to plead for us and obtain whatsoever is necessary for our salvation. Forget not our special petitions. . . . May we always be thankful to God for the blessings we have received in the past. Whatsoever we ask for the present or future, we submit to the divine will, realizing that God knows best what is good for us. We know he will respond to our prayers and petitions in one way or another. Amen.

St. Jude, pray for us!

My Jesus, mercy!

NINTH DAY

O holy St. Jude, apostle and martyr, grant that we may so dispose our lives that we may always be pleasing to God. In working out our salvation in this life we have many needs and necessities. Today we turn to you, asking you to intercede for us and obtain for us the favors we ask of God. Especially do we petition for. . . .

May we not so much seek temporal good but rather what will avail our souls, knowing that it will profit us nothing if we gain the whole world yet suffer the loss of our soul.

Therefore, may we incline ourselves toward the divine will, seeing God's good and gracious purpose in all our trials. Amen.

St. Jude, pray for us!

My Jesus, mercy!

Litany to St. Jude

(For private use only)

Lord, have mercy on us.
Christ, have mercy on us.
Lord, have mercy on us.
Christ, hear us.
Christ, graciously hear us.
God the Father of heaven,
have mercy on us.
God the Son, Redeemer of
the world, *have mercy on us.*
God the Holy Spirit, *have
mercy on us.*
Holy Trinity, one God, *have
mercy on us.*

St. Jude, relative of Jesus and
Mary,*
St. Jude, while on earth
deemed worthy to see Jesus
and Mary, and to enjoy
their company,

St. Jude, raised to the dignity
of an apostle,
St. Jude, who had the honor
of beholding your Divine
Master humble himself to
wash your feet,
St. Jude, who at the Last Supper did receive the Holy
Eucharist from the hands of
Jesus,
St. Jude, who after the profound grief which the death
of your beloved Master
caused you, had the consolation of beholding him
risen from the dead, and of
assisting at his glorious
ascension,

---
* *Pray for us.*

38

St. Jude, who was filled with the Holy Spirit on the day of Pentecost,

St. Jude, who did preach the Gospel in Persia,

St. Jude, who did convert many people to the Faith,

St. Jude, who did perform wonderful miracles in the power of the Holy Spirit,

St. Jude, who did restore an idolatrous king to health of both soul and body,

St. Jude, who did impose silence on demons, and confound their oracles,

St. Jude, who did foretell to a weak prince, an honorable peace with his powerful enemy,

St. Jude, who did take from deadly serpents the power of injuring man,

St. Jude, who, disregarding the threats of the impious, did courageously preach the doctrine of Christ,*

St. Jude, who did gloriously suffer martyrdom for the love of thy Divine Master,

Blessed apostle, with confidence, we invoke you!

Blessed apostle, with confidence, we invoke you!

Blessed apostle, with confidence, we invoke you!

St. Jude, help of the hopeless, aid me in my distress!

St. Jude, help of the hopeless, aid me in my distress!

St. Jude, help of the hopeless, aid me in my distress!

That by your intercession both priests and people of the Church may obtain an ardent zeal for the Faith of Jesus Christ, *we beseech you, hear us!*

That you would defend our Sovereign Pontiff and obtain peace and unity for the Church, *we beseech you, hear us!*

That all unbelievers may be converted to the true Faith, *we beseech you, hear us!*

That faith, hope and charity may increase in our hearts, *we beseech you, hear us!*

That we may be delivered from all evil thoughts, and from all the snares of the devil, *we beseech you, hear us!*

That you would vouchsafe to aid and protect all those who honor you, *we beseech you, hear us!*

That you would preserve us from all sin and from all occasions of sin, *we beseech you, hear us!*

* *Pray for us.*

39

That you would defend us at
the hour of death, against
the fury of the devil and his
evil spirits, *we beseech you,
hear us!*

Lamb of God, who takes
away the sins of the world,
have mercy on us.

Lamb of God, who takes
away the sins of the world,
have mercy on us.

Lamb of God, who takes
away the sins of the world,
grant us peace.

Let Us Pray

O Lord Jesus Christ, who has said, Ask and you shall receive, seek and you shall find, knock and it shall be opened unto
you, grant, we beseech you, to us who ask the gift of your most
divine love, that with all our hearts, words and works, we may
love you and never cease to praise you. Amen.

Novena to
the Immaculate Conception

Novena Prayer in Honor of
the Immaculate Conception

O Mary Immaculate, lily of purity, I salute you, because from the very first instant of your conception you were filled with grace. I thank and adore the Most Holy Trinity for having imparted to you favors so sublime. O, Mary, full of grace, help me to share, even though just a little, in the fullness of grace so wonderfully bestowed on you in your Immaculate Conception. With firm confidence in your never-failing intercession, we beseech you to obtain for us the intention of this novena . . . and also that purity of mind, heart and body necessary to unite us with God. Amen.

O Mary, conceived without sin, pray for us who have recourse to you.

O Mother of God, by your Immaculate Conception, intercede for us with your Divine Son, and obtain for us from him, the favor for which we pray. Amen.

Special Prayer for Each Day

FIRST DAY

O most Holy Virgin, who was pleasing to the Lord and became his mother, immaculate in body and spirit, in faith and in love, look kindly on me as I implore your powerful intercession. O most Holy Mother, who by your blessed Immaculate Conception, from the first moment of your conception did crush the head of the enemy, receive our prayers as we implore you to present at the throne of God the favor we now request. . . .

O Mary of the Immaculate Conception, Mother of Christ, you had influence with your Divine Son while upon earth; you have the same influence now in heaven. Pray for us and obtain for us from him the granting of my petition if it be the Divine Will. Amen.

SECOND DAY

O Mary, ever blessed Virgin, Mother of God, Queen of angels and of saints, we salute you with the most profound veneration and filial devotion as we contemplate your holy Immaculate Conception. We thank you for your maternal protection and for the many blessings that we have received through your wondrous mercy and most powerful intercession. In all our necessities we have recourse to you with unbounded confidence. O Mother of Mercy, we beseech you now to hear our prayer and to obtain for us of your Divine Son the favor that we so earnestly request in this novena. . . .

O Mary of the Immaculate Conception, Mother of Christ, you had influence with your Divine Son while upon earth; you have the same influence now in heaven. Pray for us and obtain for us from him the granting of my petition if it be the Divine Will. Amen.

THIRD DAY

O Blessed Virgin Mary, glory of the Christian people, joy of the universal Church and Mother of Our Lord, speak for us to the Heart of Jesus, who is your Son and our brother. O Mary, who by your holy Immaculate Conception did enter the world free from stain, in your mercy obtain for us from Jesus the special favor which we now so earnestly seek. . . .

O Mary of the Immaculate Conception, Mother of Christ, you had influence with your Divine Son while upon earth; you have the same influence now in heaven. Pray for us and obtain for us from him the granting of our petition if it be the Divine Will. Amen.

FOURTH DAY

O Mary, Mother of God, endowed in your glorious Immaculate Conception with the fullness of grace; unique among women in that you are both mother and virgin: Mother of Christ and Virgin of Christ, we ask you to look down with a tender heart from your throne and listen to our prayers as we earnestly ask that you obtain for us the favor for which we now plead. . . .

O Mary of the Immaculate Conception, Mother of Christ, you had influence with your Divine Son while upon earth; you have the same influence now in heaven. Pray for us and obtain for us from him the granting of our petition if it be the Divine Will. Amen.

FIFTH DAY

O Lord, who, by the Immaculate Conception of the Virgin Mary, did prepare a fitting dwelling for your Son, we beseech you that as by the foreseen death of your Son, you did preserve her from all stain of sin grant that, through her intercession, we may be favored with the granting of the grace that we seek for at this time. . . .

O Mary of the Immaculate Conception, Mother of Christ, you had influence with your Divine Son while upon earth; you have the same influence now in heaven. Pray for us and obtain for us from him the granting of our petition if it be the Divine Will. Amen.

SIXTH DAY

Glorious and immortal Queen of Heaven, we profess our firm belief in your Immaculate Conception pre-ordained for you in the merits of your Divine Son. We rejoice with you in your Immaculate Conception. To the one and ever-reigning God, Father, Son and Holy Spirit, three in one Person, one in nature, we offer thanks for your blessed Immaculate Conception. O Mother of the Word made Flesh, listen to our petition as we ask this special grace during this novena. . . .

O Mary of the Immaculate Conception, Mother of Christ, you had influence with your Divine Son while upon earth; you have the same influence now in heaven. Pray for us and obtain for us from him the granting of our petition if it be the Divine Will. Amen.

SEVENTH DAY

O Immaculate Virgin, Mother of God and my mother, from the sublime heights of your dignity turn your merciful eyes upon me while I, full of confidence in your bounty and keeping in mind your Immaculate Conception and fully conscious of your power, beg of you to come to our aid and ask your Divine Son to grant the favor we earnestly seek in this novena . . . if it be beneficial for our immortal souls and the souls for whom we pray.

O Mary of the Immaculate Conception, Mother of Christ, you had influence with your Divine Son while upon earth; you have the same influence now in heaven. Pray for us and obtain for us from him the granting of our petition if it be the Divine Will. Amen.

EIGHTH DAY

O most gracious Virgin Mary, beloved Mother of Jesus Christ, our Redeemer, intercede with him for us that we be granted the favor which we petition for so earnestly in this novena. . . . O Mother of the Word Incarnate, we feel animated with confidence that your prayers in our behalf will be graciously heard before the throne of God. O glorious Mother of God, in memory of your joyous Immaculate Conception, hear our prayers and obtain for us our petitions.

45

O Mary of the Immaculate Conception, Mother of Christ, you had influence with your Divine Son while upon earth; you have the same influence now in heaven. Pray for us and obtain for us from him the granting of our petition if it be the Divine Will. Amen.

NINTH DAY

O Mother of the King of the Universe, most perfect member of the human race, "our tainted nature's solitary boast," we turn to you as mother, advocate and mediatrix. O Holy Mary, assist us in our present necessity. By your Immaculate Conception, O Mary conceived without sin, we humbly beseech you from the bottom of our heart to intercede for us with your Divine Son and ask that we be granted the favor for which we now plead . . . .

O Mary of the Immaculate Conception, Mother of Christ, you had influence with your Divine Son while upon earth; you have the same influence now in heaven. Pray for us and obtain for us from him the granting of our petition if it be the Divine Will. Amen.

Litany of the Blessed Virgin

(Also called "The Litany of Loreto")

We fly to your patronage, O holy Mother of God, despise not our petitions in our necessities but deliver us from all dangers, O ever glorious and blessed Virgin.

Lord, have mercy on us.
Christ, have mercy on us.
Lord, have mercy on us.
Christ, hear us.
Christ, graciously hear us.
God the Father of Heaven,
   have mercy on us.
God the Son, Redeemer of
   the world, *have mercy on us.*
God the Holy Spirit, *have*
   mercy on us.
Holy Trinity, one God, *have*
   mercy on us.

Holy Mary,*
Holy Mother of God,
Holy Virgin of virgins,
Mother of Christ,
Mother of divine grace,*
Mother most pure,
Mother most chaste,
Mother inviolate,
Mother undefiled,
Mother most amiable,
Mother most admirable,
Mother of Good Counsel,
Mother of our Creator,
Mother of our Redeemer,
Virgin most prudent,
Virgin most venerable,
Virgin most renowned,
Virgin most powerful,
Virgin most merciful,
Virgin most faithful,
Mirror of justice,
Seat of wisdom,
Cause of our joy,

Spiritual vessel,
Vessel of honor,
Singular vessel of devotion,
Mystical rose,
Tower of David,
Tower of ivory,
House of Gold,
Ark of the covenant,
Gate of heaven,
Morning star,
Health of the sick,
Refuge of sinners,
Comforter of the afflicted,
Help of Christians,
Queen of Angels,
Queen of Confessors,
Queen of Patriarchs,
Queen of Prophets,
Queen of Martyrs,
Queen of Apostles,
Queen of Virgins,
Queen of All Saints,
Queen conceived without
   original sin,
Queen assumed into heaven,
Queen of the most holy Ro-
   sary,
Queen of Peace,

Lamb of God, who takes
   away the sins of the world,
   spare us, O Lord.
Lamb of God, who takes
   away the sins of the world,
   graciously hear us, O Lord.

---

* *Pray for us.*

47

Lamb of God, who takes away the sins of the world, *have mercy on us.*
Pray for us, O holy Mother of God.

That we may be made worthy of the promises of Christ.

Let Us Pray

Pour forth, we beseech Thee, O Lord, your grace into our hearts; that as we have known the Incarnation of Christ your Son by the message of an angel, so, by his Passion and Cross, we may be brought to the glory of his resurrection: through the same Christ our Lord. Amen.

Memorare

Remember, O most gracious Virgin Mary, that never was it known that anyone who fled to your protection, implored your help, and sought your intercession, was left unaided. Inspired with this confidence, I fly unto you, O virgin of virgins, my mother. To you I come, before you I stand sinful and sorrowful. O Mother of the Word Incarnate, despise not my petitions, but in your mercy hear and grant my prayer. Amen.

Novena to St. Joseph

O glorious St. Joseph, faithful follower of Jesus Christ, to you we raise our hearts and hands to implore your powerful intercession in obtaining from the benign heart of Jesus all the helps and graces necessary for our spiritual and temporal welfare, particularly for the grace of a happy death and the special favor we now request. . . .

O guardian of the Word Incarnate, we feel animated with confidence that your prayers in our behalf will be graciously heard before the throne of God.

O glorious St. Joseph, through the love you bear to Jesus Christ and for the glory of his name, hear our prayers and obtain our petitions. Amen.

FIRST DAY

O great St. Joseph, with feelings of unlimited confidence, we beg you to bless this novena that we begin in your honor. "You are never invoked in vain" says the seraphic Theresa of Jesus. Be you then to me what you have been to that spouse of the Sacred Heart of Jesus and graciously hear me as you did her. Amen.

St. Joseph, pray for us.

SECOND DAY

O blessed St. Joseph, tender-hearted father, faithful guardian of Jesus, chaste spouse of the Mother of God, we pray and beseech you to offer to God the Father, his divine Son, bathed in blood on the Cross for sinners, and through the thrice holy name of Jesus obtain for us of the eternal Father the favor for which we implore your intercession . . . .

Amid the splendors of eternity, forget not the sorrows of those who suffer, those who pray, those who weep; stay the almighty arm which smites us, that by your prayers and those of your most holy spouse, the Heart of Jesus may be moved to pity and to pardon. Amen.

St. Joseph, pray for us.

THIRD DAY

Blessed St. Joseph, enkindle in our cold hearts a spark of your charity. May God be always the first and only object of our affections. Keep our souls always in sanctifying grace and, if we should be so unhappy as to lose it, give us the strength to recover it immediately by a sincere repentance. Help us to such a love of our God as will always keep us united to him. Amen.

O glorious St. Joseph, through the love you bear to Jesus Christ and for the glory of his name, hear our prayers and obtain our petitions.

FOURTH DAY

St. Joseph, pride of heaven, unfailing hope for our lives, and support of those on earth, graciously accept our prayer of praise. You were appointed spouse of the chaste Virgin by the Creator of the world. He willed that you be called "father" of the Word and serve as agent of our salvation. May the triune God who has bestowed upon you heavenly honors, be praised forever. And may he grant us through your merits the joy of a blessed life and a favorable answer to our petition. . . . Amen.

St. Joseph, pray for us.

FIFTH DAY

O holy St. Joseph, what a lesson your life is for us, ever so eager to appear so anxious to display before the eyes of men the graces that we owe entirely to the liberality of God. In addition to the special favor for which we plead in this novena . . . grant that we may attribute to God the glory of all things, that we may love the humble and hidden life, that we may not desire any other position than the one given us by Providence and that we may always be a docile instrument in the hands of God. Amen.

St. Joseph, pray for us.

SIXTH DAY

O glorious St. Joseph, appointed by the Eternal Father as the guardian and protector of the life of Jesus Christ, the comfort and support of his Holy Mother, and the instrument in his great design for the redemption of mankind; you who had the happiness of living with Jesus and Mary, and of dying in their arms, be moved with the confidence we place in you, and procure for us from the Almighty, the particular favor which we humbly ask through your intercession. . . . Amen.

St. Joseph, pray for us.

SEVENTH DAY

O faithful and prudent St. Joseph, watch over our weakness and our inexperience; obtain for us that prudence which reminds us of our end, which directs our paths and which protects us from every danger. Pray for us, then, O great Saint, and by your love for Jesus and Mary, and by their love for you, obtain for us the favor we ask in this novena. . . . Amen.

St. Joseph, pray for us.

EIGHTH DAY

O blessed Joseph, to whom it was given not only to see and to hear that God whom many kings longed to see and saw not; to hear and heard not; but also to carry him in your arms, to embrace him, to clothe him, and to guard and defend him, come to our assistance and intercede with him to look favorably on our present petition. . . . Amen.

St. Joseph, pray for us.

NINTH DAY

O good St. Joseph, help us to be like you, gentle to those whose weakness leans on us; help us to give to those who seek our aid, succor that they may journey unafraid. Give us your faith, that we may see the right shining above the victories of might. Give us your hope that we may stand secure, untouched by doubting, steadfast to endure. Give us your love that as the years increase an understanding heart may bring us peace. Give us your purity that the hour of death finds us untouched by evil's breath. Give us your love of labor that we shirk no lot in life that calls for honest work. Give us your love of poverty so that we live contented, let wealth come or go. Give us your courage that we may be strong; give us your meekness to confess our sins. Give us your patience that we may possess the kingdom of our souls without distress. Help us, dear Saint, to live that when life ends we pass with you to Jesus and his friends.

O Glorious St. Joseph, hear our prayers and obtain our petitions. Amen.

St. Joseph, pray for us.

Litany of St. Joseph

Lord, have mercy on us.
Christ, have mercy on us.
Lord, have mercy on us.
Christ, hear us.
Christ, graciously hear us.
God the Father of Heaven,
have mercy on us.
God the Son, Redeemer of
the world, *have mercy on us.*
God the Holy Spirit, *have
mercy on us.*
Holy Trinity, one God, *have
mercy on us.*
Holy Mary, *pray for us.*

St. Joseph,*
Renowned offspring of David,
Light of patriarchs,
Spouse of the Mother of God,
Chaste guardian of the Virgin,
Foster-father of the Son of
God,
Diligent protector of Christ,
Head of the Holy Family,
Joseph most just,
Joseph most chaste,
Joseph most prudent,

———
* *Pray for us.*

Joseph most strong,
Joseph most obedient,
Joseph most faithful,
Mirror of patience,
Lover of poverty,
Model of laborers,
Glory of home life,
Guardian of virgins,
Pillar of families,
Solace of the wretched,
Hope of the sick,
Patron of the dying,
Terror of demons,
Protector of Holy Church,

Lamb of God, who takes
away the sins of the world,
spare us, O Lord.
Lamb of God, who takes
away the sins of the world,
graciously hear us, O Lord.
Lamb of God, who takes
away the sins of the world,
have mercy on us.

He made him the lord of his
household. *And prince over
all his possessions.*

Let Us Pray

O God, who in your ineffable providence did vouchsafe to choose blessed Joseph to be the spouse of your most holy Mother, grant, we beseech you, that we may have for our advocate in heaven him whom we venerate as our protector on earth, who lives and reigns world without end. Amen.

Novena to
Our Lady of Lourdes

Daily Novena Prayer
to Our Lady of Lourdes

Be blessed, O most pure Virgin, for having vouchsafed to manifest your shining with life, sweetness and beauty, in the Grotto of Lourdes, saying to the child, St. Bernadette: "I am the Immaculate Conception." A thousand times we congratulate you upon your Immaculate Conception. And now, O ever Immaculate Virgin, Mother of mercy, Health of the sick, Refuge of sinners, Comforter of the afflicted, you know our wants, our troubles, our sufferings; deign to cast upon us a look of mercy. By appearing in the Grotto of Lourdes, you were pleased to make it a privileged sanctuary, whence you dispense your favors, and already many have obtained the cure of their infirmities, both spiritual and corporal. We come, therefore, with the most unbounded confidence to implore your maternal intercession. Obtain for us, O loving Mother, the granting of our request. . . .

Through gratitude for your favors, we will endeavor to imitate your virtues, that we may one day share your glory.

Our Lady of Lourdes, Mother of Christ, you had influence with your Divine Son while upon earth. You have the same influence now in heaven. Pray for us; obtain for us from your Divine Son our special requests if it be the Divine Will. Amen.

Our Lady of Lourdes, pray for us.

St. Bernadette, pray for us.

FIRST DAY

O Mary Immaculate, Our Lady of Lourdes, virgin and mother, queen of heaven, chosen from all eternity to be the Mother of the Eternal Word and in virtue of this title preserved from original sin, we kneel before you as did little Bernadette at Lourdes and pray with childlike trust in you that as we contemplate your glorious appearance at Lourdes, you will look with mercy on our present petition and secure for us a favorable answer to the request for which we are making this novena. . . .

O brilliant star of purity, Mary Immaculate, Our Lady of Lourdes, glorious in your assumption, triumphant in your coronation, show unto us the mercy of the Mother of God. Virgin Mary, Queen and Mother, be our comfort, hope, strength and consolation. Amen.

Our Lady of Lourdes, pray for us.

St. Bernadette, pray for us.

SECOND DAY

Be blessed, O most pure Virgin, for having vouchsafed to manifest yourself shining with light, sweetness and beauty, in the Grotto of Lourdes, saying to the child, St. Bernadette: "I am the Immaculate Conception!" O Mary Immaculate, inflame our hearts with one ray of the burning love of your pure heart. Let them be consumed with love for Jesus and for you, in order that we may merit one day to enjoy your glorious eternity. O dispenser of his graces here below, take into your keeping and present to your Divine Son the petition for which we are making this novena. . . .

O brilliant star of purity, Mary Immaculate, Our Lady of Lourdes, glorious in your assumption, triumphant in your coronation, show unto us the mercy of the Mother of God. Virgin Mary, queen and Mother, be our comfort, hope, strength and consolation. Amen.

Our Lady of Lourdes, pray for us.
St. Bernadette, pray for us.

THIRD DAY

"You are all fair, O Mary, and there is in you no stain of original sin." O Mary, conceived without sin, pray for us who have recourse to you. O brilliant star of sanctity, as on that lovely day, upon a rough rock in Lourdes you spoke to the child Bernadette and a fountain broke from the plain earth and miracles happened and the great shrine of Lourdes began, so now I beseech you to hear our fervent prayer and do, we beseech you, grant us the petition we now so earnestly seek. . . .

O brilliant star of purity, Mary Immaculate, Our Lady of Lourdes, glorious in your assumption, triumphant in your coronation, show unto us the mercy of the Mother of God. Virgin Mary, Queen and Mother, be our comfort, hope, strength and consolation. Amen.

Our Lady of Lourdes, pray for us.

St. Bernadette, pray for us.

FOURTH DAY

O Immaculate Queen of heaven, we your wayward, erring children, join our unworthy prayers of praise and thanksgiving to those of the angels and saints and your own that the One, Holy and Undivided Trinity may be glorified in heaven and on earth. Our Lady of Lourdes, as you looked down with love and mercy upon Bernadette as she prayed her rosary in the grotto, look down now, we beseech you, with love and mercy upon us. From the abundance of graces granted you by your Divine Son, sweet Mother of God, give to each of us all that your motherly heart sees we need and at this moment look with special favor on the grace we seek in this novena. . . .

O brilliant star of purity, Mary Immaculate, Our Lady of Lourdes, glorious in your assumption, triumphant in your coronation, show unto us the mercy of the Mother of God. Virgin Mary, Queen and Mother, be our comfort, hope, strength and consolation. Amen.

Our Lady of Lourdes, pray for us.
St. Bernadette, pray for us.

FIFTH DAY

O Mary Immaculate, Mother of God and our mother, from the heights of your dignity look down mercifully upon us while we, full of confidence in your unbounded goodness and confident that your Divine Son will look favorably upon any request you make of him in our behalf, we beseech you to come to our aid and secure for us the favor we seek in this novena. . . .

O brilliant star of purity, Mary Immaculate, Our Lady of Lourdes, glorious in your assumption, triumphant in your coronation, show unto us the mercy of the Mother of God. Virgin Mary, Queen and Mother, be our comfort, hope, strength and consolation. Amen.

Our Lady of Lourdes, pray for us.
St. Bernadette, pray for us.

SIXTH DAY

O glorious Mother of God, so powerful under your special title of Our Lady of Lourdes, to you we raise our hearts and hands to implore your powerful intercession in obtaining from the benign Heart of Jesus all the helps and graces necessary for our spiritual and temporal welfare and for the special favor we so earnestly seek in this novena. . . . O Lady of Bernadette, with the stars of heaven in your hair and the roses of earth at your feet, look with compassion upon us today as you did so long ago on Bernadette in the Grotto of Lourdes.

O brilliant star of purity, Mary Immaculate, Our Lady of Lourdes, glorious in your assumption, triumphant in your coronation, show unto us the mercy of the Mother of God. Virgin Mary, Queen and Mother, be our comfort, hope, strength and consolation. Amen.

Our Lady of Lourdes, pray for us.

St. Bernadette, pray for us.

SEVENTH DAY

O Almighty God, who by the Immaculate Conception of the Blessed Virgin Mary did prepare a worthy dwelling place for your Son, we humbly beseech you that as we contemplate the apparition of Our Lady in the Grotto of Lourdes, we may be blessed with health of mind and body. And, O most gracious Mother Mary, beloved Mother of our Lord and redeemer, look with favor upon us as you did that day on Bernadette and intercede with him for us that the favor we now so earnestly seek may be granted to us. . . .

O brilliant star of purity, Mary Immaculate, Our Lady of Lourdes, glorious in your assumption, triumphant in your coronation, show unto us the mercy of the Mother of God. Virgin Mary, Queen and Mother, be our comfort, hope, strength and consolation. Amen.

Our Lady of Lourdes, pray for us.

St. Bernadette, pray for us.

EIGHTH DAY

O Immaculate Mother of God, from heaven itself you came to appear to little Bernadette in the rough Grotto of Lourdes! And as Bernadette knelt at your feet and the magic spring burst forth and as multitudes have knelt ever since before your shrine, O Mother of God, we kneel before you today to ask that in your mercy you plead with your Divine Son to grant the special favor we seek in this novena. . . .

O brilliant star of purity, Mary Immaculate, Our Lady of Lourdes, glorious in your assumption, triumphant in your coronation, show unto us the mercy of the Mother of God. Virgin Mary, Queen and Mother, be our comfort, hope, strength and consolation. Amen.

Our Lady of Lourdes, pray for us.

St. Bernadette, pray for us.

NINTH DAY

O glorious Mother of God, to you we raise our hearts and hands to implore your powerful intercession in obtaining from the benign heart of Jesus all the graces necessary for our spiritual and temporal welfare, particularly for the grace of a happy death. O Mother of our Divine Lord, as we conclude this novena for the special favor we seek at this time . . . we feel animated with confidence that your prayers in our behalf will be graciously heard. O Mother of my Lord, through the love you bear to Jesus Christ and for the glory of his Name, hear our prayers and obtain our petitions.

O brilliant star of purity, Mary Immaculate, Our Lady of Lourdes, glorious in your assumption, triumphant in your coronation, show unto us the mercy of the Mother of God. Virgin Mary, Queen and Mother, be our comfort, hope, strength and consolation. Amen.

Our Lady of Lourdes, pray for us.
St. Bernadette, pray for us.

Litany of Our Lady of Lourdes

(For private devotion only)

Lord, have mercy on us.
Christ, have mercy on us.
Lord, have mercy on us.
Christ, hear us.
Christ, graciously hear us.
God the Father of Heaven, *have mercy on us.*
God the Son, redeemer of the world, *have mercy on us.*
God the Holy Spirit, *have mercy on us.*
Holy Trinity, one God, *have mercy on us.*

Exalted model of all mothers, Our Lady of Lourdes,*
Mother who did suffer so much,
Mother poor and without shelter,

Mother who did bear along forgotten roads the fruit of your womb,
Who did find no other shelter for your Son and our God than a wild cave, and no other cradle than a manger,
Who did declare—"I am the Immaculate Conception,"
Who did appear to an humble peasant girl in order to teach us humility,
Who was clad in a white robe to remind us of purity,
Who did wear a girdle of blue to remind us of heaven,
Who did tread on a rosebush

---
* *Pray for us.*

62

to remind us of the sufferings we must endure in order to merit heaven,

Who did carry the rosary to induce us to pray,

Who had your hands joined and your eyes raised to heaven to draw us to penance,

Who is the Star of Hope,

Who prays to the Sacred Heart of Jesus for us,

Who gives strength to the clergy,

Who heals the sick,

Who is the health of the weak,

Refuge of sinners,

Comforter of the afflicted.

Our Lady of Lourdes, conceived without sin, *pray for us who have recourse to you.*

Lamb of God, who takes away the sins of the world, *spare us, O Lord.*

Lamb of God, who takes away the sins of the world, *graciously hear us, O Lord.*

Lamb of God, who takes away the sins of the world, *have mercy on us.*

Pray for us, Our Lady of Lourdes, Holy Mother of God.

That we may be made worthy of the promises of Christ.

Prayer

Our Lady of Lourdes, so fruitful in miracles, protect, with that hand which nothing can resist, our Holy Father the Pope. Infuse into us the spirit of faith, hope and charity. We all believe the truth of your apparitions, and the unlimited power with which your Divine Son has armed you. Hence it is that we have recourse to you.

Hymn to Our Lady of Lourdes

Ave, Ave, Ave Maria!
Ave, Ave, Ave Maria!

Immaculate Mary!
Our hearts are on fire.

That title so wondrous
Fills all our desires!

We pray for God's glory,
May His Kingdom come;
We pray for His vicar,
Our Father, and Rome.

We pray for our Mother,
The Church upon earth;
And bless, sweetest Lady,
The land of our birth.

O Mary! O Mother!
Be Queen of our land;
May we be your children
Guided by your hand!

May we be your children
And souls that now stray
From Jesus and Mary
In heresy's way.

For poor, sick, afflicted,
Your mercy we crave;
And comfort the dying,
You light of the grave!

Rosary Novena

The 54 day Rosary Novena consists of the daily recitation of five decades of the Rosary for twenty-seven days in petition and five decades for twenty-seven days in thanksgiving.

The Rosary is composed of fifteen decades, each decade consisting of one Our Father, ten Hail Marys, and one Glory Be to the Father, recited in honor of some mystery in the life of our Lord and of his Blessed Mother.

Prayer of Petition

(To be said for the first 27 days)

O Glorious Mother of God, Queen of the most holy Rosary, I beseech you to accept this Rosary Novena which, as a crown of roses, I lay at your feet. As I offer this prayer, most gracious Lady, I earnestly ask you to intercede for me with your Divine Son so that I may be granted the favor which I now seek through your powerful intercession. . . .

Prayer of Thanksgiving

(To be said for the second 27 days)

O Glorious Mother of God, Queen of the most holy Rosary, I kneel in gratitude before you to offer in thanksgiving this Rosary Novena which as a crown of roses I lay at your feet. O most gracious Lady, I am truly grateful for your powerful intercession in behalf of the favor I so earnestly sought and have received. O Mother of God, keep me always under your special protection. Amen.

The Joyful Mysteries

First Mystery—The Annunciation

Meditation: Let us contemplate in this mystery how the angel Gabriel saluted our Blessed Lady, "Full of Grace," and declared to her the Incarnation of our Lord Jesus Christ.

Say: One Our Father, Ten Hail Marys, One Glory Be to the Father.

Prayer: O Holy Mary, Queen of Virgins, by the most high mystery of the Incarnation of your beloved Son, our Lord Jesus Christ, by which our salvation was so happily begun, obtain for us light to understand the benefit he has bestowed in vouchsafing to become our brother, and in giving us you, his own most beloved Mother, to be our Mother also. Amen.

I pray for the gift of the virtue of Humility.

Second Mystery—The Visitation

Meditation: Let us contemplate in this mystery how the Blessed Virgin Mary, understanding from the angel that her cousin, St. Elizabeth, had conceived, went with haste into the mountains of Judea, to visit her, and remained with her three months.

Say: One Our Father, Ten Hail Marys, One Glory Be to the Father.

Prayer: O Holy Virgin, most spotless mirror of humility, by the exceeding charity which moved you to visit your holy cousin, St. Elizabeth, obtain that our hearts may be spiritually visited by your most holy Son, and that, being purified from sin, we may praise and bless him forever. Amen.

I pray for the gift of the virtue of Charity.

Third Mystery—The Nativity

Meditation: Let us contemplate in this mystery how the Blessed Virgin Mary, when the time of her delivery

67

was come, brought forth our Redeemer, Jesus Christ, at midnight, and laid him in a manger, because there was no room for him in the inns at Bethlehem.

Say: One Our Father, Ten Hail Marys, One Glory Be to the Father.

Prayer: O most pure Mother of God, by your exceeding happiness in being chosen to give birth to the Savior of the world, I beseech you to obtain for me grace to lead so pure and holy a life, that I may hereafter eternally sing the mercies of your Son and his benefits to us, through you. Amen.

I pray for the gift of the virtue of
Poverty.

Fourth Mystery—The Presentation

Meditation: Let us contemplate in this mystery how the most Blessed Virgin Mary, on the day of her purification, presented the child Jesus in the Temple where holy Simeon, giving thanks to God, received him with great devotion into his arms.

Say: One Our Father, Ten Hail Marys, One Glory Be to the Father.

Prayer: O Holy Virgin, most admirable mistress and pattern of obedience, who did present in the Temple the Lord of the Temple, obtain that, with holy Simeon

and devout Anna, we may praise and glorify him forever. Amen.

I pray for the gift of the virtue of
Obedience.

Fifth Mystery—The Finding of the Child Jesus in the Temple

Meditation: Let us contemplate in this mystery how
the Blessed Virgin Mary, having lost her beloved Son
in Jerusalem, sought him for the space of three days,
and at length found him the fourth day in the Temple,
in the midst of the doctors, disputing with them, being
then but twelve years old.

*Say: One Our Father, Ten Hail Marys, One
Glory Be to the Father.*

Prayer: Most Blessed Virgin, more than martyr in
your sufferings, and yet the comfort of the afflicted, by
the unspeakable joy which filled your soul on finding
your beloved Son in the Temple, disputing with the
doctors, obtain that we may so effectually seek as to
find him, and never be separated from him.

I pray for the gift of the virtue of
Piety.

Say: The "Hail, Holy Queen," as on p. 113.

Let Us Pray

O God, whose only-begotten Son, by his life, death, and resurrection, has purchased for us the rewards of eternal life, grant, we beseech you, that meditating on these mysteries in the most holy Rosary of the Blessed Virgin Mary, we may imitate what they contain, and obtain what they promise through Christ our Lord. Amen.

The Sorrowful Mysteries

First Mystery—The Agony of Our Blessed Savior in the Garden

Meditation: Let us contemplate in this mystery how our Blessed Savior was so afflicted for us in the garden of Gethsemani, that his body was bathed in a bloody sweat, which ran trickling down in great drops to the ground.

Say: One Our Father, Ten Hail Marys, One Glory Be to the Father.

Prayer: Most holy Virgin, more than martyr, by that fervent prayer which your most beloved Son poured forth to his Father in the garden, vouchsafe to intercede for us, that we may always and in all things conform and subject ourselves to the will of God. Amen.

I pray for the gift of the virtue of
Contrition.

Second Mystery—The Scourging of Our Lord at the Pillar

Meditation: Let us contemplate in this mystery how our Lord Jesus Christ was most cruelly scourged by Pilate's order, receiving, as was revealed to St. Bridget, about five thousand stripes.

Say: One Our Father, Ten Hail Marys, One Glory Be to the Father.

Prayer: O Mother of God, overflowing fountain of patience, by the stripes your beloved Son vouchsafed to endure for us, obtain for us grace to mortify our rebellious senses, and with that sword of grief which pierced your most tender soul, to cut off all occasions of sin. Amen.

I pray for the gift of the virtue of Purity.

Third Mystery—The Crowning of Our Savior with Thorns

Meditation: Let us contemplate in this mystery how those cruel ministers of Satan plaited a crown of sharp thorns, and most cruelly pressed it on the most sacred head of our Lord Jesus Christ.

Say: One Our Father, Ten Hail Marys, One Glory Be to the Father.

Prayer: O Mother of the eternal King of Glory, by those sharp thorns wherewith his holy head was pierced, we beseech you that by your intercession we may be delivered here from all motions of pride and in the day of judgment from that confusion which our sins deserve. Amen.

I pray for the gift of the virtue of
Courage.

Fourth Mystery—Jesus Carries His Cross

Meditation: Let us contemplate in this mystery how our Lord Jesus Christ, being sentenced to die, bore with great patience the cross which was laid upon him for his greater torment and ignominy.

*Say: One Our Father, Ten Hail Marys, One
Glory Be to the Father.*

Prayer: O Holy Virgin, example of patience, by the most painful carrying of the cross on which your Son, our Lord Jesus Christ, bore the heavy weight of our sins, obtain of him for us, by your intercession, courage and strength to follow his steps, and bear our cross after him to the end of our lives. Amen.

I pray for the gift of the virtue of
Patience.

Fifth Mystery—The Crucifixion

Meditation: Let us contemplate in this mystery how our Lord Jesus Christ, having come to Mount Calvary, was stripped of his clothes, and his hands and feet most cruelly nailed to the cross, in the presence of his most afflicted Mother.

Say: One Our Father, Ten Hail Marys, One Glory Be to the Father.

Prayer: O Holy Mary, Mother of God, as the body of your beloved Son was for us extended on the cross, so may our desires be daily more and more stretched out in his service, and our hearts wounded with compassion for his most bitter passion. Do you, O most Blessed Virgin, graciously vouchsafe to help us to accomplish the work of our salvation by your powerful intercession. Amen.

I pray for the gift of the virtue of
Self-Denial.

Say: The "Hail, Holy Queen," as on p. 113.

Let Us Pray

O God, whose only-begotten Son, by his life, death, and resurrection, has purchased for us the rewards of eternal life, grant, we beseech you, that meditating on these mysteries in the most holy Rosary of the Blessed Virgin Mary, we may imitate what they contain, and obtain what they promise through Christ our Lord. Amen.

The Glorious Mysteries

First Mystery—The Resurrection

Meditation: Let us contemplate in this mystery how our Lord Jesus Christ, triumphing gloriously over death, rose again the third day, immortal and impassible.

> *Say: One Our Father, Ten Hail Marys, One Glory Be to the Father.*

Prayer: O glorious Virgin Mary, by the unspeakable joy you did feel at the resurrection of your beloved Son, we beseech you to obtain that our hearts may never go astray after the false joys of this world, but may be ever and wholly employed in the pursuit of the only true and solid joys of heaven. Amen.

> I pray for the gift of the virtue of Faith.

Second Mystery—The Ascension

Meditation: Let us contemplate in this mystery how our Lord Jesus Christ, forty days after his resurrection, ascended into heaven, attended by angels, in the sight of his most holy Mother, his apostles and disciples, to the great admiration of them all.

Say: One Our Father, Ten Hail Marys, One Glory Be to the Father.

Prayer: O Mother of God, comfort of the afflicted, as your beloved Son, when he ascended into heaven, lifted up his hands and blessed his apostles, so vouchsafe, most holy Mother, to lift up your pure hands to him for us, that we may enjoy the benefit of his blessing here on earth, and hereafter in heaven. Amen.

I pray for the gift of the virtue of
Hope.

Third Mystery—The Descent of the Holy Spirit

Meditation: Let us contemplate in this mystery how our Lord Jesus Christ, being seated on the right hand of God, sent, as he had promised, the Holy Spirit upon the apostles, who, after his ascension, continued in prayer at Jerusalem, in company with the Blessed Virgin, expecting the performance of his promise.

Say: One Our Father, Ten Hail Marys, One Glory Be to the Father.

Prayer: O Blessed Virgin, tabernacle of the Holy Spirit, we beseech you to obtain that the heavenly

Comforter, whom your beloved Son sent on his apostles to replenish them with spiritual joy, may teach us in this world the true way of salvation, and strengthen us to walk in the path of virtue and good works. Amen.

> I pray for the gift of the virtue of
> Love.

Fourth Mystery—The Assumption

Meditation: Let us contemplate in this mystery how the glorious Virgin, twelve years after the resurrection of her Son, passed out of this world unto him, and was by him assumed into heaven, accompanied by the holy angels.

> *Say: One Our Father, Ten Hail Marys, One*
> *Glory Be to the Father.*

Prayer: O most prudent Virgin, who by your entrance into the heavenly palace did fill the angels with joy and man with hope, vouchsafe to intercede for us at the hour of death, that, free from the illusions and temptations of the devil, we may joyfully and successfully pass out of this temporal state to enjoy the happiness of eternal life. Amen.

> I pray for the gift of the virtue of
> Eternal Happiness.

Fifth Mystery—The Coronation of the Blessed Virgin

Meditation: Let us contemplate in this mystery how the Blessed Virgin Mary was crowned by her Son with the brightest diadem of glory, to the great exultation of the whole court of heaven and the particular triumph of the saints.

> *Say: One Our Father, Ten Hail Marys, One Glory Be to the Father.*

Prayer: O Glorious Queen of all the heavenly citizens, we beseech you to accept this Rosary, which as a crown of roses we lay at your feet; and grant, most gracious Lady, that by your intercession our souls may be inflamed with so ardent a desire to see you so gloriously crowned, that it may never die in us until it be changed into the happy fruition of your blessed sight. Amen.

> I pray for the gift of the virtue of Devotion to Mary.

> *Say: The "Hail, Holy Queen," as on p. 113.*

Let Us Pray

O God, whose only-begotten Son, by his life, death, and resurrection, has purchased for us the rewards of eternal life, grant, we beseech you, that meditating on these mysteries in the most holy Rosary of the Blessed Virgin Mary, we may imitate what they contain, and obtain what they promise through Christ our Lord. Amen.

Novena to St. Ann

Glorious St. Ann, filled with compassion for those who invoke you, with love for those who suffer, heavily laden with the weight of my troubles, I kneel at your feet and humbly beg you to take my present need under your special protection. (*Here mention request.*) Vouchsafe to recommend it to your daughter, the Blessed Virgin Mary, and lay it before the throne of Jesus. Cease not to intercede for me until my request is granted. Above all, obtain for me the grace of one day meeting my God face to face, and with you and Mary and all the saints praising him through all eternity. Amen.

FIRST DAY

Great St. Ann, engrave indelibly on my heart and in my mind the words that have reclaimed and sanctified so many sinners: "What shall it profit a man to gain the whole world if he lose his own soul?" May this be the principal fruit of these prayers by which I will strive to honor you during this Novena. At your feet I renew my resolution to invoke you daily, not only for the success of my temporal affairs and to be preserved from sickness and suffering, but above all, that I may be preserved from all sin, that I may succeed in working out my eternal salvation and that I will receive the special grace of (*name it*). O most powerful St. Ann, do not let me lose my soul, but obtain for me the grace of winning my way to heaven, there with you, your blessed spouse and your glorious daughter, to sing the praise of the most holy and adorable Trinity forever and ever. Amen.

Our Father, Hail Mary, and Glory Be to the Father.

Pray for us, St. Ann.
That we may be made worthy of the promises of Christ.

SECOND DAY

Glorious St. Ann, how can you be otherwise than overflowing with tenderness toward sinners like myself, since you are the grandmother of him who shed his blood for them, and the mother of her whom the saints call the advocate of sinners? To you, therefore, I address my prayers with confidence. Vouchsafe to commend me to Jesus and Mary so that, at your request, I may be granted remission of my sins, perseverance, the love of God, charity for all mankind, and the special grace (*name it*) of which I stand in need at the present time. O most powerful protectress, let me not lose my soul, but obtain for me that through the merits of Jesus Christ and the intercession of Mary, I may have the happiness of seeing them, of loving and praising them with you for all eternity. Amen.

Our Father, Hail Mary, and Glory Be to the Father.

Pray for us, St. Ann.
That we may be made worthy of the promises of Christ.

THIRD DAY

Beloved of Jesus, Mary and Joseph, mother of the Queen of Heaven, take us and all who are dear to us under your special care. Obtain for us the virtues you instilled into the heart of her who was destined to become the Mother of God, and the graces with which you were endowed. Sublime model of Christian womanhood, pray that we may imitate your example in our homes and families, listen to our petitions, and obtain our request (*name it*). Guardian of the infancy and childhood of the most Blessed Virgin Mary, obtain the graces necessary for all who enter the marriage state, that imitating your virtues they may sanctify their homes and lead the souls entrusted to their care to eternal glory. Amen.

Our Father, Hail Mary, and Glory Be to the Father.

Pray for us, St. Ann.
That we may be made worthy of the promises of Christ.

Glorious Saint, I kneel in confidence at your feet, for you also have tasted the bitterness and sorrow of life. My necessities, the cause of my tears, are (*name them*). Good St. Ann, you who did suffer much during the twenty years that preceded your glorious maternity, I beseech you, by all your sufferings and humiliations, to grant my prayer. I pray you, through your love for your glorious spouse, through your love for your immaculate child, through the joy you did feel at the moment of her happy birth, not to refuse me. Bless me, bless my family and all who are dear to me, so that some day we may all be with you in the glory of heaven, for all eternity. Amen.

Our Father, Hail Mary, and Glory Be to the Father.

Pray for us, St. Ann.
That we may be made worthy of the promises of Christ.

FIFTH DAY

Great Saint, how far I am from resembling you. I so easily give way to impatience and discouragement; and so easily give up praying when God does not at once grant my request. Prayer is the key to all heavenly treasures and I cannot pray, because my weak faith and lack of confidence fail me at the slightest delay of divine mercy. O my powerful protectress, come to my aid, listen to my petition for (*name it*), make my confidence and fervor, supported by the promises of Jesus Christ, redouble in proportion as the trial to which God in his goodness subjects me is prolonged, that I may obtain like you more than I can venture to ask for. In the future I will remember that I am made for heaven and not for earth; for eternity and not for time; that consequently I must ask, above all, the salvation of my soul which is assured to all who pray properly and who persevere in prayer. Amen.

Our Father, Hail Mary, and Glory Be to the Father.

Pray for us, St. Ann.
That we may be made worthy of the promises of Christ.

SIXTH DAY

Glorious St. Ann, mother of the Mother of God, I beg you to obtain through your powerful intercession the pardon of my sins and the assistance I need in my troubles (*name it*). What can I not hope for if you deign to take me under your protection? The Most High has been pleased to grant the prayers of sinners, whenever you have been charitable enough to be their advocate.

Kneeling at your feet, I beg you to help me in all spiritual and temporal dangers; to guide me in the true path of Christian perfection, and finally to obtain for me the grace of ending my life with the death of the just, so that I may contemplate face to face your beloved Jesus and your daughter Mary in your loving companionship throughout eternity. Amen.

Our Father, Hail Mary, and Glory Be to the Father.

Pray for us, St. Ann.
That we may be made worthy of the promises of Christ.

SEVENTH DAY

O good St. Ann, so justly called the mother of the infirm, the cure of those who suffer from disease, look kindly upon the sick for whom I pray; alleviate their sufferings; cause them to sanctify their sufferings by patience and complete submission to the divine will; finally deign to obtain health for them and with it the firm resolution to honor Jesus, Mary and yourself by the faithful performance of duties. But, merciful St. Ann, I ask you above all for the salvation of my soul, rather than bodily health, for I am convinced that this fleeting life is given us solely to assure us a better one. Now, we cannot obtain that better life without the help of God's graces. I earnestly beg them of you for the sick and for myself, especially the petition for which I am making this novena (*name it*) through the merits of our Lord Jesus Christ, through the intercession of his Immaculate Mother and through your efficacious and powerful mediation. O glorious St. Ann, Amen.

Our Father, Hail Mary, Glory Be to the Father.

Pray for us, St. Ann.
That we may be made worthy of the promises of Christ.

Remember, O St. Ann, you whose name signifies grace and mercy, that never was it known that anyone who fled to your protection, implored your help and sought your intercession was left unaided. Inspired with this confidence, I fly unto you, good and kind mother; I take refuge at your feet and, sinful as I am, I venture to appear before you, burdened with the weight of my sins. O holy mother of the Immaculate Virgin Mary, despise not my petition (*name it*) but hear me and grant my prayer. Amen.

Our Father, Hail Mary, Glory Be to the Father.

Pray for us, St. Ann.
That we may be made worthy of the promises of Christ.

NINTH DAY

Most holy mother of the Virgin Mary, glorious St. Ann, I, a miserable sinner, confiding in your kindness, choose you today as my special advocate. I offer and consecrate my person and all my interests to your care and maternal solicitude. I hope to serve and honor you all my life for the love of your most holy daughter and to do all in my power to spread devotion to you.

O my very good mother and advocate, deign to accept me as your servant, and to adopt me as your child. O glorious St. Ann, I beg you, by the passion of my most loving Jesus, the Son of Mary, your most holy daughter, to assist me in all the necessities both of my body and my soul. Venerable Mother, I beg you to obtain for me the favor I seek in this novena (*name it*) and the grace of leading a life perfectly conformable in all things to the divine will. I place my soul in your hands and in those of your kind daughter. I confide it to you, above all at the moment when it will be about to separate itself from my body in order that, appearing under your patronage before the Supreme Judge, he may find it worthy of enjoying his divine presence in your holy companionship in heaven. Amen.

Our Father, Hail Mary, Glory Be to the Father.

Pray for us, St. Ann.
That we may be made worthy of the promises of Christ.

Litany in Honor of St. Ann

(For Private Devotion)

Lord, have mercy on us.
Christ, have mercy on us.
Lord, have mercy on us.
Christ, hear us.
Christ, graciously hear us.
God the Father of Heaven, *have mercy on us.*
God the Son, Redeemer of the world, *have mercy on us.*
God the Holy Spirit, *have mercy on us.*
Holy Trinity, one God, *have mercy on us.*

St. Ann,*
St. Ann, Mother of the Virgin Mary,

St. Ann, Spouse of St. Joachim,
St. Ann, Ark of Noah,
St. Ann, Ark of the Covenant,
St. Ann, Joy of Angels,
St. Ann, Grace of Patriarchs,
St. Ann, Oracle of Prophets,
St. Ann, Praise of All Saints,
St. Ann, Mirror of Obedience,
St. Ann, Mirror of Patience,
St. Ann, Mirror of Compassion,
St. Ann, Mirror of Devotion,
St. Ann, Mirror of Piety,

---
* *Pray for us.*

St. Ann, Bulwark of the Church,
St. Ann, Deliverer of Captives,
St. Ann, Mother of Widows,
St. Ann, Mother of Virgins,
St. Ann, Mother of the Sick,
St. Ann, Light of the Blind,
St. Ann, Tongue of the Dumb,
St. Ann, Hearing of the Deaf,
St. Ann, Comforter of the Afflicted,
St. Ann, never invoked without answer,

Lamb of God, who takes away the sins of the world, *spare us, O Lord.*
Lamb of God, who takes away the sins of the world, *graciously hear us, O Lord.*
Lamb of God, who takes away the sins of the world, *have mercy on us.*
Pray for us, St. Ann.
That we may be made worthy of the promises of Christ.

Let Us Pray

O God, who did vouchsafe to endow blessed St. Ann with grace that she was found worthy to be the mother of her who brought forth your only-begotten Son, grant in your grace, that we who devoutly honor her memory, may through her prayers attain everlasting life, through Jesus Christ our Lord. Amen.

Novena to St. Anthony

Novena Prayer to St. Anthony

O wonderful St. Anthony, glorious on account of the fame of your miracles, and through the condescension of Jesus in coming in the form of a little child to rest in your arms, obtain for me of his bounty the grace which I ardently desire from the depths of my heart. . . . You who were so compassionate toward miserable sinners, regard not the unworthiness of those who pray to you, but the glory of God that it may be once again magnified by the granting of the particular request . . . which I now ask for with persevering earnestness. Amen.

One Our Father, one Hail Mary and one Glory Be to the Father, in honor of St. Anthony.
St. Anthony, pray for us.

FIRST DAY

O holy St. Anthony, gentlest of saints, your love for God and charity for his creatures made you worthy while on earth to possess miraculous powers. Miracles waited on your word, which you were ever ready to speak for those in trouble or anxiety. Encouraged by this thought, I implore you to obtain for me the favor I seek in this novena. . . . The answer to my prayer may require a miracle; even so, you are the saint of miracles. O gentle and loving St. Anthony, whose heart was ever full of human sympathy, whisper my petition into the ears of the Infant Jesus, who loved to be folded in your arms, and the gratitude of my heart will always be yours.

Our Father, Hail Mary, Glory Be to the Father.
St. Anthony, pray for us.

SECOND DAY

O miracle-working St. Anthony, remember that it never has been heard that you have left without help or relief anyone who in his need had recourse to you. Animated now with the most lively confidence, even with full conviction of not being refused, I fly for refuge to thee, O most favored friend of the Infant Jesus. O eloquent preacher of the divine mercy, despise not my supplications but, bringing them before the throne of God, strengthen them by your intercession and obtain for me the favor I seek in this novena. . . .

Our Father, Hail Mary, Glory Be to the Father.
St. Anthony, pray for us.

THIRD DAY

O purest St. Anthony, who through your angelic virtue was made worthy to be caressed by the Divine Child Jesus, to hold him in your arms and press him to your heart, I entreat you to cast a benevolent glance upon me. O glorious St. Anthony, born under the protection of Mary Immaculate, on the Feast of her Assumption into heaven, and consecrated to her and now so powerful an intercessor in heaven, I beseech you to obtain for me the favor I ask in this novena. . . . O great wonder-worker, intercede for me that God may grant my request.

Our Father, Hail Mary, Glory Be to the Father.
St. Anthony, pray for us.

FOURTH DAY

I salute and honor you, O powerful helper, St. Anthony. The Christian world confidently turns to you and experiences your tender compassion and powerful assistance in so many necessities and sufferings that I am encouraged in my need to seek your help in obtaining a favorable answer to my request for the favor I seek in this novena. . . . O holy St. Anthony, I beseech you, obtain for me the grace that I desire.

Our Father, Hail Mary, Glory Be to the Father.
St. Anthony, pray for us.

FIFTH DAY

I salute you, St. Anthony, lily of purity, ornament and glory of Christianity. I salute you, great Saint, cherub of wisdom and seraph of divine love. I rejoice at the favors our Lord has so liberally bestowed on you. In humility and confidence I entreat you to help me, for I know that God has given you charity and pity, as well as power. I ask you by the love you did feel toward the Infant Jesus as you held him in your arms to tell him now of the favor I seek through your intercession in this novena . . . .

Our Father, Hail Mary, Glory Be to the Father.
St. Anthony, pray for us.

SIXTH DAY

O glorious St. Anthony, chosen by God to preach his Word, you received from him the gift of tongues and the power of working the most extraordinary miracles. O good St. Anthony, pray that I may fulfill the will of God in all things so that I may love him, with you, for all eternity. O kind St. Anthony, I beseech you, obtain for me the grace that I desire, the favor I seek in this novena . . . .

Our Father, Hail Mary, Glory Be to the Father.
St. Anthony, pray for us.

SEVENTH DAY

O renowned champion of the faith of Christ, most holy St. Anthony, glorious for your many miracles, obtain for me from the bounty of my Lord and God the grace which I ardently seek in this novena . . . . O holy St. Anthony, ever attentive to those who invoke you, grant me the aid of your powerful intercession.

Our Father, Hail Mary, Glory Be to the Father.
St. Anthony, pray for us.

EIGHTH DAY

O holy St. Anthony, you have shown yourself so powerful in your intercession, so tender and so compassionate toward those who honor you and invoke you in suffering and distress. I beseech you most humbly and earnestly to take me under your protection in my present necessities and to obtain for me the favor I desire. . . . Recommend my request to the merciful Queen of Heaven, that she may plead my cause with you before the throne of her Divine Son.

Our Father, Hail Mary, Glory Be to the Father.
St. Anthony, pray for us.

NINTH DAY

St. Anthony, servant of Mary, glory of the Church, pray for our Holy Father, our bishops, our priests, our Religious Orders, that, through their pious zeal and apostolic labors, all may be united in faith and give greater glory to God. St. Anthony, helper of all who invoke you, pray for me and intercede for me before the throne of Almighty God that I be granted the favor I so earnestly seek in this novena. . . .

Our Father, Hail Mary, Glory Be to the Father.
St. Anthony, pray for us.

May the divine assistance remain always with us. Amen.

May the souls of the faithful departed, through the mercy of God, rest in peace. Amen.

O God, may the votive commemoration of blessed Anthony, your confessor, be a source of joy to your Church, that she may always be fortified with spiritual assistance, and deserve to enjoy eternal rewards. Through Christ our Lord. Amen.

Litany of St. Anthony

Lord, have mercy on us.
Christ, have mercy on us.
Lord, have mercy on us.
Christ, hear us.
Christ, graciously hear us.

Holy Mary,*
St. Anthony of Padua,
St. Anthony, martyr in desiring to die for Christ,
St. Anthony, pillar of the Church,
St. Anthony, worthy priest of God,
St. Anthony, apostolic preacher,
St. Anthony, teacher of truth,

St. Anthony, hammer of heretics,
St. Anthony, comforter of the afflicted,
St. Anthony, helper in necessities,
St. Anthony, deliverer of captives,
St. Anthony, guide of the erring,
St. Anthony, restorer of lost things,
St. Anthony, chosen intercessor,
St. Anthony, continuous worker of miracles,

* Pray for us.

92

Be merciful unto us, spare us, O Lord.

Be merciful unto us, graciously hear us, O Lord.

From all evil, *O Lord, deliver us.*

From all sin,**

From all dangers of body and soul,

From the snares of the devil,

From pestilence, famine and war,

From eternal death,

Through the merits of St. Anthony,***

Through his zeal for the conversion of sinners,

Through his desire for the crown of martyrdom,

Through his fatigues and teaching,

Through his penitential tears,

Through his patience and humility,

Through his glorious death,

Through the number of his prodigies,

In the day of judgment, we sinners,***

That Thou wouldst vouchsafe to bring us to true penance,

That Thou wouldst vouchsafe to assist us in our necessities,

That Thou wouldst vouchsafe to grant our petitions,

That Thou wouldst vouchsafe to kindle the fire of divine love within us,

That Thou wouldst vouchsafe us the protection and intercession of St. Anthony,

Son of God,

Lamb of God, who takes away the sins of the world, *spare us, O Lord.*

Lamb of God, who takes away the sins of the world, *graciously hear us, O Lord.*

Lamb of God, who takes away the sins of the world, *have mercy on us.*

Christ, hear us.

Christ, graciously hear us.

Pray for us, St. Anthony.

That we may be made worthy of the promises of Christ.

---

* *Pray for us.*
** *O Lord, deliver us.*
*** *We beseech you, hear us.*

Novena to the
Little Flower

O St. Theresa of the Child Jesus, who during your short life on earth became a mirror of angelic purity, of love strong as death, and of wholehearted abandonment to God, now that you rejoice in the reward of your virtues, cast a glance of pity on me as I leave all things in your hands. Make my troubles your own, speak a word for me to our Lady Immaculate, whose flower of special love you were—to that Queen of Heaven "who smiled on you at the dawn of life." Beg her as Queen of the heart of Jesus to obtain for me by her powerful intercession the grace I yearn for so ardently at this moment . . . and that she join with it a blessing that may strengthen me during life, defend me at the hour of death, and lead me straight on to a happy eternity. Amen.

O God, who did inflame with your Spirit of Love, the soul of your servant, Therese of the Child Jesus, grant that we also may love you and make you much loved. Amen.

O Theresa of the Child Jesus, well beloved and full of charity, in union with you, I reverently adore the majesty of God; and since I rejoice with exceeding joy in the singular gifts of grace bestowed upon you during your life, and your gifts of glory after death, I give him deepest thanks for them; I beseech you with all my heart's devotion to be pleased to obtain for me, by your effectual intercession, above all things, the grace of a holy life and a happy death. Moreover, I beg of you to obtain for me. . . . But if what I ask of you so earnestly does not tend to the glory of God and the greater good of my soul, do you, I pray, obtain for me that which is more profitable to both these ends. Amen.

St. Theresa of the Child Jesus, pray for us.

SECOND DAY

Almighty God, giver of all good gifts, who did will that Blessed Theresa, being watered by the heavenly dew of your guiding grace, should bloom in Carmel with the beauty of virginity and patience in suffering, grant that I your servant may go forward in the order of her sweetness and may be found worthy to become a devoted and loyal follower of Christ. Amen.

St. Theresa of the Child Jesus, pray for us.

THIRD DAY

O St. Theresa of the Child Jesus, lily of purity, ornament and glory of Carmel, I greet you, great saint, seraph of divine love. I rejoice in the favors our Lord so liberally bestowed on you. In humility and confidence I ask you to help me, for I know that God has given you love and pity as well as power. Tell him, now, I beseech you, of the favor I seek in this novena . . . . Your request will crown my petition with success and bring joy to my heart. Remember your promise to do good on earth: "I shall spend my heaven doing good on earth. After death I shall let fall a shower of roses."

St. Theresa of the Child Jesus, pray for us.

FOURTH DAY

O Little Flower of Jesus, who at an early age had your heart set on Carmel and in your brief earthly life did become a mirror of angelic purity, of courageous love and of wholehearted surrender to Almighty God, turn your eyes of mercy upon me who trusts in you. Obtain for me the favor I seek in this novena . . . and the grace to keep my heart and mind pure and clean. O dear saint, grant me to feel in every need the power of your intercession; help to comfort me in all the bitterness of this life and especially at its end, that I may be worthy to share eternal happiness with you in heaven. Amen.

St. Theresa of the Child Jesus, pray for us.

FIFTH DAY

O Little Flower of Carmel, Almighty God endowed you, consumed by love for him, with wondrous spiritual strength to follow the way of perfection during the days of your short life. Sickness touched you early but you remained firm in faith and prayer was your life. O pray for me that I may benefit by your intercession and be granted the favor I ask in this novena . . . .

St. Theresa of the Child Jesus, pray for us.

SIXTH DAY

O Little Flower of Jesus, you have shown yourself so powerful in your intercession, so tender and compassionate toward those who honor you and invoke you in suffering and distress, that I kneel at your feet with perfect confidence and beseech you most humbly and earnestly to take me under your protection in my present necessity and to obtain for me the favor I ask in this novena. . . . Vouchsafe to recommend my request to Mary, the merciful Queen of Heaven, that she may plead my cause with you before the throne of Jesus, her divine Son. Cease not to intercede for me until my request is granted.

St. Theresa of the Child Jesus, pray for us.

SEVENTH DAY

Theresa of the Child Jesus, most loving saint, in union with you I adore the divine Majesty. My heart is filled with joy at the remembrance of the marvelous favors with which God blessed your life on earth and of the great glory that came to you after death. In union with you, I praise God, and offer him my humble tribute of thanksgiving. I implore you to obtain for me, through your powerful intercession, the greatest of all blessings—that of living and dying in the state of grace. I also beg of you to secure for me the special favor I seek in this novena. . . .

St. Theresa of the Child Jesus, pray for us.

EIGHTH DAY

O glorious St. Theresa, who, burning with the desire of increasing the glory of God, invariably attended to the sanctification of your own soul by the constant practice of prayer and charity so that, becoming in the Church a model of holiness, you are now in heaven the protector of all those who have recourse to you in faith, look down upon me who invokes your powerful patronage and join your petition to mine that I be granted the favor I seek in this novena. . . .

St. Theresa of the Child Jesus, pray for us.

NINTH DAY

O St. Theresa, seraphic virgin, beloved spouse of our crucified Lord, you who on earth did burn with a love so intense toward your God and my God, and now glow with a bright and purer flame in paradise, obtain for me, I beseech you, a spark of that same holy fire which shall help me to put the things of the world in their proper place and live my life always conscious of the presence of God. As I conclude my novena I also beg of you to secure for me the special favor I seek at this time . . . .

St. Theresa of the Child Jesus, pray for us.

Litany of the Little Flower of Jesus

Lord, have mercy on us.
Christ, have mercy on us.
Lord, have mercy on us.
Christ, hear us.
Christ, graciously hear us.
God the Father of Heaven,
have mercy on us.
God the Son, Redeemer of
the world, *have mercy on us.*
God the Holy Spirit, *have
mercy on us.*
Holy Trinity, one God, *have
mercy on us.*

Holy Mary,*
Our Lady of Victory,
Little Therese, servant of God,
Little Therese, victim of the
merciful love of God,
Little Therese, spouse of Jesus,
Little Therese, gift of heaven,
Little Therese, remarkable in
childhood,
Little Therese, an example of
obedience,
Little Therese, resigned to the
Divine Will of God,
Little Therese, lover of peace,
Little Therese, lover of pa-
tience,
Little Therese, lover of gentle-
ness,
Little Therese, heroic in sacri-
fices,*
Little Therese, generous in
forgiving,

Little Therese, benefactress of
the needy,
Little Therese, lover of Jesus,
Little Therese, devoted to the
Holy Face,
Little Therese, consumed with
Divine love of God,
Little Therese, advocate of ex-
treme cases,
Little Therese, persevering in
prayer,
Little Therese, a powerful ad-
vocate with God,
Little Therese, showering
roses,
Little Therese, doing good
upon earth,
Little Therese, answering all
prayers,
Little Therese, lover of holy
chastity,
Little Therese, lover of volun-
tary poverty,
Little Therese, lover of obe-
dience,
Little Therese, burning with
zeal for God's glory,
Little Therese, inflamed with
the spirit of love,
Little Therese, child of bene-
diction,
Little Therese, perfect in sim-
plicity,

---

* *Pray for us.*

Little Therese, so remarkable
for trust in God,
Little Therese, gifted with un-
usual intelligence,
Little Therese, never invoked
without some answer,
Little Therese, teaching us the
sure way,
Little Therese, victim of Divine Love,

Lamb of God, who takes
away the sins of the world,
spare us, O Lord.

Lamb of God, who takes
away the sins of the world,
graciously hear us, O Lord.
Lamb of God, who takes
away the sins of the world,
have mercy on us.

Little Flower of Jesus, pray
for us.

*Without a
Divinity there
is for man
neither purpose,
goal, nor hope,
only a
trembling future,
an eternal fear
of the dark.*

Jean Paul

General Prayers

The Holy Rosary

The Rosary is a devotion to the Incarnation of Our Lord and to his Blessed Mother. It is composed of fifteen decades, each decade consisting of one Our Father, ten Hail Marys, and one Glory Be to the Father, each being recited in honor of some mystery in the life of our Lord and of his Blessed Mother. During each decade we should call to mind the mystery that it is intended to honor, and pray that we may learn to practice the virtue specially taught us by that mystery.

I—The Five Joyful Mysteries

1. The Annunciation
2. The Visitation
3. The Nativity
4. The Presentation
5. The Finding in the Temple

II—The Five Sorrowful Mysteries

1. The Agony in the Garden
2. The Scourging at the Pillar
3. The Crowning with Thorns
4. The Carrying of the Cross
5. The Crucifixion

III—The Five Glorious Mysteries

1. The Resurrection
2. The Ascension
3. The Coming of the Holy Spirit on the Apostles
4. The Assumption of the Blessed Virgin
5. The Coronation of the Blessed Virgin

The Way of the Cross

Preparatory Prayer

O Lord, at this time I want to think of your journey to Calvary. You went along this way out of obedience to the Father and out of love for me. You took upon yourself the heavy cross to atone for my sins and to redeem the world. In these thoughts on your passion let me be grateful for so great a love. Mary, Mother of Sorrows, accompany me along this way.

1. *Jesus Is Condemned to Death*

   Your will, O God, is supreme. May my one great purpose be to seek it and to follow it.

2. *Jesus Receives the Cross*

   Grant, O divine Savior, that I may faithfully fulfill every duty for love of you.

3. *Jesus Falls the First Time under the Cross*

How many times, O Lord, have I been faithless through sin to you?

4. *Jesus Is Met by his Blessed Mother*

Mary, my mother, intercede for me with your Divine Son.

5. *The Cross Is Laid Upon Simon of Cyrene*

Every time I put temptation aside and resist sin, I help you, Jesus, to carry your cross.

6. *Veronica Wipes the Face of Jesus*

Your suffering was for me. I will not desert you, but always defend you.

7. *Jesus Falls the Second Time*

Forgive me, O merciful Lord, my many, my repeated sins.

8. *Jesus Speaks to the Women of Jerusalem*

Your words of mercy and pardon give me fresh hope and confidence.

9. *Jesus Falls the Third Time*

May my sins never discourage me, but lead me to seek more and more your help.

10. *Jesus Is Stripped of His Garments*

I will be your valiant follower. May my conduct never shame you before men.

11. *Jesus Is Nailed to the Cross*

Your commands mean that I should conquer every unholy desire. I will conquer in your name.

12. *Jesus Dies on the Cross*

When my hour comes, may I die bravely, dear Jesus, for you.

13. *Jesus Is Taken Down from the Cross*

Wherever I am, you, O Lord, will be my true, though unseen companion.

14. *Jesus Is Laid in the Sepulchre*

You, my eternal God, will I always serve. With you I live, and with you I die.

Prayers for Special Occasions

Prayer for Light

O Holy Spirit of God, take me as your disciple: guide me, illuminate me, sanctify me. Bind my hands that they may do no evil; cover my eyes that they may see it no more; sanctify my heart that evil may not dwell within me. Be you my God; be you my guide. Wherever you lead me I will go; whatever you forbid me I will renounce; and whatever you command me in your strength I will do. Lead me, then, unto the fullness of your truth. Amen.

Prayer for All in Trouble

Most blessed Virgin, in your life of glory, remember the sorrows of earth. Look with kindness on those who suffer, who struggle against difficulties, who drink unceasingly the bitterness of this life. Have pity on those who love each other and are separated. Have pity on the lonely of heart. Have pity on the weakness of our faith. Have pity on the objects of our affection. Have pity on those who weep, those who pray, those who fear. Obtain for all, hope and peace. Amen.

Act of Spiritual Communion

My Jesus, I believe in you; I hope in you; I love you. I am heartily sorry for all my sins. Come into my heart, cleanse it, purify it, and remain there forever. My Lord, Jesus Christ, preserve my soul unto life everlasting.

For Our Own Beloved Dead

Good Jesus, whose loving Heart was ever troubled by the sorrows of others, look with pity on the souls of our dear ones in purgatory. O you, who "loved your own," hear our cry for mercy, and grant that those whom you called from our homes and hearts, may soon enjoy everlasting rest in the home of your love in heaven. Eternal rest, grant unto them, O Lord, and let perpetual light shine on them. May their souls and the souls of all the faithful departed, through the mercy of God, rest in peace. Amen.

Prayer before the Crucifix

Look down upon me, good and gentle Jesus, while before your face I humbly kneel, and with burning soul, pray and beseech you to fix deep in my heart lively sentiments of faith, hope and charity, true contrition for my sins, and a firm purpose of amendment; while I contemplate, with great love and tender pity, your five most precious wounds, pondering over them within me, calling to mind the words which David, your Prophet, said of you, my Jesus: "They have pierced my hands and my feet, they have numbered all my bones."

Prayer after Holy Communion

My God, enable me to bear you, for you alone can. Cleanse my heart and mind from all that is past. Wipe out clean all my recollections of evil. Rid me from all langor, sickness, irritability, feebleness of soul. Give me a true perception of things unseen, and make me truly, practically, and in the details of my life, prefer you to anything on earth, and the future world to the present. Give me a true instinct determining between right and wrong, humility in all things, and a tender, longing love for you. (Cardinal Newman)

Prayer in Affliction

O Lord, keep me from bitterness. It is so easy to nurse sharp bitter thoughts each dull dark hour! Against self-pity, Man of Sorrows, defend me with your deep understanding and your gentle power! And out of all this hurt of pain and heartbreak help me to harvest a new sympathy for suffering humankind; a wiser pity for those who lift a heavier cross with you.

Salve Regina

Hail! Holy Queen, Mother of Mercy, our life, our sweetness, and our hope! To you do we cry, poor banished children of Eve; to you do we send up our sighs, mourning and weeping in this valley of tears. Turn then, most gracious advocate, your eyes of mercy toward us, and after this our exile show unto us the blessed Fruit of your womb, Jesus. O clement, O loving, O sweet Virgin Mary; pray for us, O holy Mother of God, that we may be made worthy of the promises of Christ. Amen.

Prayer for Priests

O Jesus, Eternal Priest, keep your priests within the shelter of your Sacred Heart, where none may touch them. Keep unstained their anointed hands, which daily touch your Sacred Body. Keep unsullied their lips, daily purpled with your Precious Blood. Keep pure and unworldly their hearts sealed with the sublime mark of the priesthood. Let your holy love surround them from the world's contagion. Bless their labors with abundant fruit, and may the souls to whom they minister be their joy and consolation here and their everlasting crown hereafter. Mary, Queen of the Clergy, pray for us; obtain for us numerous and holy priests.

Prayer for a Happy Death

O God, who has doomed all men to die, but has concealed from all the hour of their death, grant that I may pass my days in the practice of holiness and justice, and that I may deserve to quit this world in the peace of a good conscience, and in the embrace of your love through the same Christ our Lord. Amen.

Prayer for All in Military Service

O God, we beseech you, watch over the souls of all who are exposed to the horrors of war, and to the spiritual dangers inseparable from a military life. Bless them with such a strong faith that no human respect may ever lead them to deny it, or fear to practice it. Do you by your grace fortify them against the contagion of bad example. Keep them always in your friendship. May nothing in life or death ever separate them from you. Amen.

Let Me Bring Love

O God, make me an instrument of peace,
that I may bring love where there is hate;
that I may pardon where there is guilt;
that I may unite where there is dissension;

that I may bring truth where there is error;
that I may bring faith where there is darkness;
that I may bring joy where there is suffering;
that I may seek;
not to be comforted, but to bring comfort;
not to be understood, but to understand;
not to be loved, but to love; this alone is impor-
    tant.
For when we give, we receive;
when we pardon, we are forgiven;
when we die, we enter new life. Amen.

Prayer for Enlightenment

Come, Holy Spirit, enlighten the darkness of my understanding and sharpen my conscience, so that I may recognize God's will in all things. Send forth your light and truth into my soul! May I see all my sins and failures in this light and confess them with a contrite heart. Jesus Christ gentle Savior, I put my hope of salvation in you. Accept my confession with loving mercy and move my heart to true sorrow for my sins. Heavenly Father, when you look into my soul, look not so much at the evil I have done but at the genuine sorrow that I feel within my heart. Help me to confess all my sins with a childlike trust in your loving forgiveness. Amen.

Prayer for the Souls in Purgatory

O Divine Heart of Jesus, grant, we beseech you, eternal rest to the souls in purgatory, the final grace to those who shall die today, true repentance to sinners, the light of faith to pagans, and your blessing to me and mine. To you, O most compassionate Heart of Jesus, I commend all these souls, and I offer to you on their behalf all the merits, together with the merits of your most holy Mother and of all the saints and angels, and all the sacrifices of the Holy Mass, Communions, prayers and good works, which shall be accomplished today throughout the Christian world. Amen.

Act of Resignation

My Lord God, even now resignedly and willingly, I accept at your hands with all its anxieties, pains and sufferings whatever kind of death it may please you to be mine. Amen.

Prayer for the Restoration of Things Lost and Stolen

O Blessed St. Anthony! The grace of God has made you a powerful advocate in all necessities and the patron for the restoration of things lost or stolen. To you I turn today with childlike love and heartfelt confidence. O how many thousands have you miraculously aided in the recovery of lost goods! You were the counselor of the erring, the comforter of the afflicted, the healer of the sick, the raiser of the dead, the deliverer of the captive, the refuge of the afflicted. To you do I hasten, O Blessed St. Anthony! Help me in my present affliction. I recommend what I have lost to your care in the secure hope that you will restore it to me if it be to the greater glory of God and to the spiritual benefit of my soul. Obtain also for me an active faith, peace of mind, disgust for the vain pleasures of the world, and an ardent desire for the imperishable goods of eternity. Amen.

Prayer of St. Patrick

Christ, as a light, illumine and guide me!
Christ, as a shield, o'ershadow and cover me.
Christ, be under me! Christ be over me.
Christ, be beside me on left hand and right.
Christ, be before me, behind me, about me.
Christ, this day be within and without me.
Christ, the lowly and the meek.
Christ, the all powerful, be in the heart of each to
    whom I speak.
In the mouth of each who speaks to me
In all who draw near me, or see me, or hear me.
    Amen.

Disciple's Prayer

O Holy Spirit of God,
take me as your disciple;
guide me, enlighten me, sanctify me.
Bind my hands that they may do no evil,

cover my eyes, that they may see it no more,
sanctify my heart
that evil may not dwell within me.
Be my God; be my guide.
Wherever you lead me, I will go.
Whatever you forbid me I will renounce
Whatever you command me,
in your strength I will do.
Lead me, then to the fullness
of your truth. Amen.

House Blessing

Visit, O Lord, we beseech you this home; and drive far from it all snares of the enemy. Let your holy angels dwell herein to preserve us in peace, and may your blessing be always upon us through Christ our Lord. Amen.

May the divine assistance remain always with us. And may the souls of the faithful departed, through the mercy of God, rest in peace. Amen.

Prayer for a Happy Death

Grant us, O Lord, always to follow the example of your holy family, that at the hour of our death your glorious Virgin Mother with blessed Saint Joseph may come to meet us, and so we may deserve to be received by you into your everlasting dwelling place. Amen.

Anima Christi

Soul of Christ, sanctify me.
Body of Christ, save me.
Blood of Christ, inebriate me.
Water from the side of Christ, wash me.
Passion of Christ, strengthen me.
O good Jesus, hear me.
Within your wounds, hide me.
Permit me not to be separated from you.
From the malignant enemy, defend me.
On the hour of my death, call me,
And bid me come to you!
That with your saints I may praise you,
forever and ever. Amen.

Act of Sorrow

Forgive me my sins, O Lord, forgive me my sins;
the sins of my age, the sins of my youth, the sins of my
soul, the sins of my body; my idle sins, my serious
voluntary sins, the sins I know, the sins I have concealed so long, and which are now hidden from my
memory.

I am truly sorry for every sin, mortal and venial,
for all the sins of my childhood up to the present hour.

I know my sins have wounded your tender heart,
O my Savior, let me be freed from the bonds of evil
through the most bitter passion of my Redeemer.

O my Jesus, forget and forgive what I have
been. Amen.

Prayer for Patience

Lord Jesus Christ, temper my impatience! I get excited so easily. I am so prone to anger. Let me see things in their true perspective. When others are unfair to me, let me find my justice in you. If others are hard and heartless, let me find love in you. When difficulties block my path, let me recall that your divine providence has sent them. Guide me with your spirit. Amen.

Prayer of St. Ignatius

Lord, teach me to be generous. Teach me to serve you as you deserve, to give and not to count the cost, to fight and not to heed the wounds, to toil and not to seek for rest, to labor and not ask for reward save that of knowing that I am doing your will. Amen.

Prayer of Cardinal Newman

Lord Jesus, let me never for an instant forget that you have established on earth a kingdom of your own, that the Church is your work, your establishment, your instrument, that we are under your will, your laws and your eye, that when the Church speaks you speak. Let not familiarity with this wonderful truth lead me to be insensitive to it, let not the weakness of your human representatives lead me to forget that it is you who speak and are through them. Amen.

Almighty God you have called my son/daughter to yourself. Comfort me in my sorrow; let me feel the presence of your love. Help me to overcome my sorrow as I fulfill my duties in life. Through the passion of your Son and the intercession of the Blessed Virgin Mary grant that one day I may be united with my son/daughter to you for all eternity. Amen.

Ejaculations

O Lord, be merciful to me, a sinner.

Lord, increase our faith.

My Jesus, mercy!

O Jesus, friend of the little ones, bless the children of the whole world.

Dear Jesus, hear my prayers and pour the abundance of your graces on those I love.

Heart of Jesus, once in agony, have mercy on the dying.

121

Heart of Jesus, I place my trust in you; for though I fear all things from my weakness, I hope for all things from your mercy.

The Divine Praises

Blessed be God!
Blessed be his Holy Name!
Blessed be Jesus Christ, true God and true Man!
Blessed be the name of Jesus!
Blessed be his most Sacred Heart!
Blessed be his most Precious Blood!
Blessed be Jesus in the most holy Sacrament of the Altar!
Blessed be the Holy Spirit, the Paraclete!
Blessed be the great Mother of God, Mary most holy!
Blessed be her holy and Immaculate Conception!
Blessed be her glorious Assumption!
Blessed be the name of Mary, Virgin and Mother!
Blessed be St. Joseph, her most chaste spouse!
Blessed be God in his angels and in his saints!

From the Scriptures

For everything there is a season,
    and a time for every matter under heaven:
A time to be born, and a time to die;
A time to plant, and a time to pluck up what is planted;
A time to kill, and a time to heal;

A time to break down, and a time to build up,
A time to weep, and a time to laugh;
A time to mourn, and a time to dance;
A time to cast away stones, and a time to gather
stones together;
A time to embrace, and a time to refrain from
embracing;
A time to seek, and a time to lose;
A time to keep, and a time to cast away;
A time to rend, and a time to sew;
A time to keep silent, and a time to speak;
A time to love, and a time to hate;
A time for war, and a time for peace.
What gain has the worker from his toil?

Ecclesiastes 3

Train up a child in the way he should go,
    and when he is old he will not depart from it.

Proverbs 21

To you, O God of my fathers,
    I give thanks and praise.

Daniel 2

How great are his signs,
    how mighty his wonders!
His kingdom is an everlasting kingdom,
    and his dominion is from generation to genera-
        tion.

Daniel 4

From the Psalms

The Lord is my shepherd, I shall not want;
    he makes me lie down in green pastures.
He leads me beside still waters;
    he restores my soul.
He guides me in paths of righteousness
    for his name's sake.

Even though I walk through the valley of the
    shadow of death,
    I fear no evil;
for you are with me;
    your rod and your staff,
    they comfort me.

You prepare a table before me
    in the presence of my enemies;
You anoint my head with oil,
    my cup overflows.
Surely goodness and mercy shall follow me
    all the days of my life;
and I shall dwell in the house of the Lord forever.

Psalm 23

Let my heart rejoice in your salvation;
    let me sing of the Lord,
"He has been good to me."

Psalm 12

Hear, O God, my cry;
   listen to my prayer!
From the earth's end I call to you
   as my heart grows faint.

Psalm 60

Hear my prayer, O Lord;
   let my cry come to you!
Do not hide your face from me
   in the day of my distress!
Incline your ear to me;
   answer me speedily on the day when I call!

Psalm 102

I will give thanks to the Lord with my whole
    heart;
   I will tell of all your wonderful deeds.
I will be glad and exult in you,
   I will sing praise to your name, O Most High.

Psalm 9

To you, O Lord, I lift up my soul,
   O my God, in you I trust.

Psalm 25

The Lord is my light and my salvation;
   whom shall I fear?

The Lord is the stronghold of my life;
    of whom shall I be afraid?

Psalm 27

O Lord, our Lord,
    how majestic is your name in all the earth!

Psalm 7

May God be gracious to us and bless us
    and make his face to shine upon us.

Psalm 67

Let the words of my mouth and the meditations
    of my heart
be acceptable in your sight,
O Lord, my rock and my redeemer.

Psalm 19

Bless the Lord, O my soul!
    O Lord, my God, you are great indeed!

Psalm 103

Probe me, O God, and know my heart;
    try me, and know my thoughts;

See if my way is crooked,
   and lead me in the way of old.

Psalm 138

When I call, answer me, O my good God,
   you who relieve me when I am in distress;
Have pity on me, and hear my prayer!

Psalm 4